MW00325043

HISTORIC
TAVERNS
of
RHODE ISLAND

HISTORIC
TAVERNS
|||||||||||||||||||||||||||||||| *of* ||||||||||||||||||||||||||||||||
RHODE ISLAND

Robert A. Geake

THE
History
PRESS

Published by The History Press
Charleston, SC 29403
www.historypress.net

Front cover images, left to right: The Pilgrim Inn, photo by author; postcard of Market Square, from the author's collection; the Brayton/Holden Tavern, photo by author; Old Pidge House, photo by Frank Farley; and postcard of the Kingston Inn, courtesy of Providence Public Library.
Back cover images, left to right: The White Horse Tavern, photo by author; postcard of the Hoyle Tavern, from the author's collection; and the Golden Ball Inn, courtesy of the Warwick Historical Society.

First published 2012

ISBN 978.1.5402.3150.5

Library of Congress CIP data applied for.

Notice: The information in this book is true and complete to the best of our knowledge. It is offered without guarantee on the part of the author or The History Press. The author and The History Press disclaim all liability in connection with the use of this book.

CONTENTS

ACKNOWLEDGEMENTS

This work began from a love of old houses and the deep appreciation that has grown over the years for the efforts of preservationists past and present in my own state of Rhode Island and throughout New England. As a young man in Providence, I strode along those streets of preserved eighteenth-century houses and absorbed as much detail as I could to enhance the histories I was reading As such, I was fortunate to be afforded an extraordinary sense of the evolution of a colonial American port city. Without the efforts of Antoinette Downing and the resolve of the Providence Preservation Society, that life-shaping experience would have been lost to myself and so many others, and so it seems fitting to begin my acknowledgements there.

As with any history, this work could not have been written without those earlier chroniclers of taverns and the life that surrounded them in early Rhode Island. I hope the reader of this book will peruse the bibliography and read a few of those titles as well.

I also want to acknowledge the associates and staff of the John Carter Brown Library at Brown University for their continued support and the privilege of presenting an early chapter of this work at their long-standing Fellows Luncheon.

The reference staff at the main branch of the Providence Public Library was especially helpful in locating some sources and images of historic buildings, and I want to thank librarian Beth Curran for her time and efforts. I must also acknowledge the reference staff of the Pawtucket Public Library for their help in reviewing, once again, the Johnson research files for this work.

Acknowledgements

The collection of images and articles on taverns in the Warwick Historical Society, compiled by Felicia Castiglioni Gardella, and the volunteers at the society, was of inestimable value to me in composing several of these chapters, and their continued support for my research is also deeply appreciated.

I want to thank, especially, Henry A.L. and Ann Eckert Brown for their support. I also want to thank Dan Santos and his volunteers at Historic New England; the Rhode Island Historical Society; the Smithfield Preservation Society; the Western Rhode Island Historical Society; the Free-Will Baptist Church of Chepachet, for its archives; and the staff of the archives department at Pawtucket City Hall.

Individually, I would like to acknowledge Jeff Saraceno and Hannah Cassilly of The History Press for their editorial assistance and support. I want to thank historian Christian McBurney for his careful reading and thoughtful recommendations, as well as James M. Allen for his photographic assistance. Last, but never least, I would like to thank my wife, Cindy, who shared many a journey in search of these old houses and whose enthusiasm for this work was a source of great confidence throughout its creation.

Chapter 1

ORDINARIES AND HOUSES OF "PUBLICK ENTERTAINMENT"

By 1647, Rhode Island had discovered, as Plymouth and Boston had before, that once settled with charter in hand, lands within the territory would become subject to waves of new immigrants, speculators and opportunists of all kinds during its formative years.

The colony founded by Roger Williams had the additional benefit of being open to freethinkers and individualists, as well as those other brands of early Americans that filled New England's shores in the early seventeenth century. As a system of self-governance was established within the first townships and the needs of the people within those townships considered, one of the first priorities was to establish a meetinghouse or a home wherein public business could be conducted, whether it be council meetings, hearings of local jurisdiction or trials when necessary. At times, such houses also served as the jail while waiting for the assembly of a town council for a hearing or the arrival of a circuit judge, when the trial was often held in the tavern's "publick room."

In the burgeoning village of Portsmouth in 1639, the town council decreed that Will Balston "shall erect and set up a house of Entertainment, for strangers, and also brew beare and to sell wine, beere, or strong liquers."

In some communities, a central house would be designated the place of meetings. Such was the case with the Captain Valentine Whitman House where the town council of Smithfield held its first meeting in 1730 and which also served as a place of muster for the early Smithfield Rangers. The Whitman House is a "stone-ender," a house with one wall built entirely

Valentine Whitman House, circa 1636. Great Road, Lincoln, Rhode Island. *Photo by author.*

Eleazer Arnold House, circa 1693. Great Road, Lincoln, Rhode Island. *Photo by author.*

of stone, encompassing the chimney, and allowing fireplaces on two floors instead of one, in a central room. Having been built along Great Road in 1694, Whitman's house served these roles well into the eighteenth century and still stands today.

Another surviving stone-ender, just a few miles down the Great Road, is the Eleazer Arnold House, which also served as an early ordinary for travelers. Built in 1693, the house was likely a long-standing ordinary before 1710, when Providence granted Arnold "licence and liberty to keep a publick house of Entertainment in said Providence Township at your dwelling, for the entertaining of Strangers, Travelers & other Persons, bothe horse and foote."[1]

"The Stone Chimney House," as Mary Caroline Crawford called the Eleazer Arnold House, was unusually spacious for its time:

> *It had four rooms on the lower floor, and on the second floor were two chambers, one of which contained a fireplace. The living room was large and commodious with its huge fireplace, the great "summer" beam upon which the guns were wont to be placed, and over the fireplace a strong*

Lower chamber of Eleazer Arnold House. *Photo by author, courtesy of Historic New England.*

eye-bolt to which could be attached a block and tackle to aid in hauling great logs to the fire.

These stone-enders were unique to Rhode Island where great quantities of building stone and lime could be found. Built in what would be called the village of Limerock, these houses of such unique design were constructed from a simple pairing of the materials available to early settlers and the necessity of a sturdy structure that would provide protection from the long winters. Inside, rooms were arranged one behind the other so that the hearths were side by side, one serving each room, hall and kitchen.[2]

Eleazer Arnold was to have a distinguished career as a judge in Providence Township and apparently took his license as a tavern keeper seriously, welcoming all travelers. When the judge died and his estate was taken into account, the belongings included "an old bed that Indians used to lie on with sum [*sic*] tobacco."

Rhode Island differed distinctly from the Puritan authority in granting licenses for "ordinaries" or "houses of publick entertainment" in that it did not cast so watchful an eye over the public gatherings in such places. One had to be "a man in good standing," that is, a man of property with the means to conduct such an establishment. The precedent for such places must surely have been in the colony for some time before the General Assembly passed a law in 1647 prohibiting the keeping of a tavern without a license under penalty of a fine of "twenty shillings to be paid to the poore." The need for ordinaries in each town grew as the population increased, and commerce and roads improved within that community and those surrounding it. The General Assembly issued licenses until 1663, but then, as it was customary of the colony to allow its towns wide freedom in dealing with their local affairs, it referred the licensing for such houses to the local governing councils.

Although less stringent than Massachusetts laws, Providence, like other colonial port towns, "acted most vigorously against the disorderly house."

In the license granted to Mary Pray of Providence, we find the injunction not to "suffer any unlawful game to be used in yr house nor an evill rule to be kept therin but doe behave yourself according to ye laws established."

One Othniel Gorton kept a tavern at Mashantatuck, near Providence, and was brought before the court by Moses Bartlet on evidence obtained that the tavern keeper had broken the law. An informant named Samuel Wescott had told Bartlet that he was at Gorton's on July 12 (it being the Sabbath) with friends and "saw said Gorton selling strong drink and entertaining people playing nine pins." Apparently, the party was later moved down the street to a friend of Gorton's, where Wescott witnessed "like disorderly wicked doings."

There were also strict provisions against serving liquor to slaves and Native Americans, and in some cases, it was even prohibited to allow them "entertainment." As early as 1640, Portsmouth had declared that those Native Americans within its community "shall not be Ideling about nor in our howses"[3] and imposed strict fines on citizens found allowing such activity. These issues were especially enforced in Charlestown, where one Thomas Addams was evicted from the town for allowing Indians "to resort together" in his house.

Another "Molato Fellow" named Isaac Dick was named in a complaint by the Indian Council as a man whose family kept a disorderly house,[4] serving liquor to "peoples Servants" as well as the Native Americans in the town.[5]

Rural villages within Rhode Island concentrated jurisdiction on Individuals rather than tavern keepers, though some placed certain responsibilities on the proprietors as well as the citizens for ferreting out "common drunkards."

In Warwick, a set of stocks was ordered to be built close to the David Arnold tavern to dissuade revelers from drunkenness. Other communities soon followed suit.

EARLY PROVIDENCE

The colony enacted its first legislation in 1647, and though some taverns had long existed on the fringes of Providence Plantations, the town's first license was granted to Goodman Mowry in 1655 to keep a house of entertainment, and he was directed to "sett out a convienient signe at ye most perspicuous place of ye said house thereby to give notice to strangers that it is a house of Entertainment."

The Mowry Tavern was the site of political gatherings, protests and religious observances of the followers of Roger Williams, and it was the site of an infamous murder early in its long history, but we will explore that episode in another chapter. An early description of the house relates that the tavern "consisted of but the 'fire room' with an enormous stone chimney, filling almost one entire side of the apartment, leaving room for a steep flight of stairs to the loft above."

Other early tavern keepers in Providence were Epenelus Olney William Turpin and John Whipple. According to Thomas Bicknell's *History of Rhode Island*, "the Turpin Inn at the west side of Towne Street just north of Hewes Street, was the largest house in town until the Court House was built, and was the meeting place of the General Assembly and the county courts before 1730."

Not all taverns were large structures capable of holding such assemblies. Many throughout Providence County and Rhode Island communities were, as the name implies, ordinary houses where a traveler could find a meal, drink and, if need be, a bed.

For those who owned property in an advantageous location, opening their houses to travelers was simply a way to earn extra income by renting a bed for the night and selling the excess ale and cider pressed at home for their own use.

John Whipple had been granted a license to keep such a "house of entertainment" in 1674. His house became a popular resort for some time. When he died in 1685, the inventory of his estate shows that it was a humble tavern indeed, consisting only of "ye lower room" and "ye chamber." The house contained a modest amount of furniture, including "three broken joint stools and a court cubbard."

Another early entrepreneur was Steven Jackson, who built a large stone-ender and a toll gate at the junction of the Kings Highway and Connecticut turnpike, just outside of Providence, in 1641. The house became known as the Ox Tavern (see Chapter 3). Though but two miles from the settlement, the old roads leading to the tavern were still largely tree-canopied lanes with just a few houses and farms spread out over long distances.

Jackson would certainly have known William Blackstone, the "sage of the wilderness." Blackstone had come to New England in 1623 but grew intolerant of his Puritan neighbors' practices, and he eventually settled fifty miles from Boston at a place he named "Study Hill." Blackstone reputedly planted the first apple orchard in the state.

A friend recollected that "he had the first of that sort called yellow sweetings that were…the richest and most delicious apple of the whole kind." He was a voracious reader, a legal scholar and an itinerant Anglican minister who, despite some theological differences, became fast friends with Roger Williams and was often invited to preach to Williams's followers. To "encourage his younger hearers," Blackstone "gave them the first apples they ever saw."

William Blackstone became a well-known figure, often seen riding a massive white bull with book in hand, as the beast lumbered into Providence.

The tavern changed hands over several generations, from Jackson to John Morey and then Philip Ester, and it doubled in size before being acquired by Jeremiah Sayles, in whose family the tavern would stay for the next 150 years. A 1902 guide to the state describes the old house and reveals that little had changed over the years. The guide gives us a glimpse into the colonial tavern's interior:

> *The building contains many colonial relics, a long beam runs lengthwise through the house, a fixture of colonial construction known as "the summer tree." In the corner of the old common room or bar room is a closet used for serving ales and liquors. It has a half door, a narrow serving shelf, and a broader shelf within. In the latter is a slot through which coins were dropped supposedly into a half bushel basket. Behind the bar room is the kitchen with a well preserved old oven. The house also contains some furniture of its halcyon days.*

By 1717, Providence had also issued licenses to William Harris, Benjamin Potter, John House, William Edmunds, John Potter, John Guile, and Thomas Parker among others, for a total of thirteen houses for publick entertainment

Old postcard of the Hoyle Tavern. *From the author's collection. Photo by James Allen.*

within the city. Fees for a license depended on the situation of the tavern or inn. The town council ordered on March 10, 1721, that the rate be set at twenty shillings for those "that liues adjoining to the Town Street [now North and South Main Streets], and those others that are Remote from said Town att the time of there taking there license shall pay downe the sum of fifteen shillings money-at the expiration of the year each person shall pay enough to make up 40 shillings."

By August 1724, the town council voted that "each person that is licensed to keepe a tavern in the Town Row shall pay the sum of 50 shillings down…and those that are licensed in the woods shall pay the sum of forty shillings downe." The "woods" at this time were but a mile or so from the center of Providence.

One of the more celebrated taverns that operated within the city was opened by Obidiah Brown in 1739 after he had obtained his license to keep "a publick ale house." The tavern soon became a popular stop for farmers coming into the city, as well as a stagecoach inn and a place where "young bloods" gathered at the neighborhood bar.

Within a few years, the house and license were purchased by Colonel Joseph Hoyle, who gave the tavern the name by which it was known thereafter. As was noted by historian Horace Belcher, Hoyle made his tavern "the leading one on the west side of town where taverns were numerous, especially on the road which is now Westminster Street, and one of the best known and popular houses in the Colony."

Hoyle retired as a tavern keeper in 1796 and died just four years later, but his tavern carried on through a succession of owners and renovations. A third story was added to the structure, and then in 1876, an ell was added, giving the now-named "Hoyle Hotel" a total of forty-five rooms for occupancy. The tavern and hotel doubtless held many memorable moments within their walls, but perhaps the most notorious occurred on the evening of December 31, 1843.

On that evening, Amas Sprague Sr., a highly respected textile manufacturer in nearby Cranston, was murdered. The Hoyle Tavern, or rather its patrons, would soon become embroiled in the trial that followed. Among the patrons at the Hoyle that night was John Gordon, and through nefarious means, he soon became a suspect in the crime. Gordon's brother Nicholas owned a tavern in Knightsville that was frequented by Sprague's employees, much to the consternation of the owner. Six months before his murder, Sprague had used his own and his prominent family's influence to have Gordon's liquor license removed. The fact that Gordon and his brothers were Irish Catholic was played out in local papers at a time when both immigration and the Catholic Church were under a firestorm of racist rhetoric in broadsheets and political speeches. The Gordon brothers, including a third brother named William, were all put on trial. Patrons from the Hoyle testified that John Gordon "came to the tavern on the night of the murder and bought drinks for the crowd several times, and kept talking about what time it was and how long he had been there, thus laying the foundation for an alibi in case he was suspected of the murder." In the end, only John was convicted and hanged for the murder. The case against and hanging of John Gordon stirred deep controversy among the state's population. Seven years after the hanging, Rhode Island abolished the death penalty, and 150 years after the trial, thanks in great part to the tenacity of historian Patrick Conley, the wrongly convicted Rhode Islander was awarded justice. On June 29, 2011, Governor John Chafee pardoned John Gordon.

BEYOND PROVIDENCE

Just north of the city, houses were also being opened for the growing traffic on the Post Road and along the Blackstone River. From *The History of Pawtucket*, published in 1878, we find the following notation:

Early drawing of the Ballou Tavern from Edward Field's *History of Pawtucket, 1902.*

Sketch of the Benedict Arnold Tavern. *Courtesy of the Warwick Historical Society.*

Ordinaries and Houses of "Publick Entertainment"

Tradition tells of an old tavern that once stood on the western side of the Blackstone River, close to the old ford. It afforded entertainment to many a traveler in those early days...Another of these ancient public houses...bore the name of the Martin House. It was originally built for a private residence by one Captain Comstock, but it subsequently was converted into a tavern and presided over by Mr. Constant Martin. The sign placed in front of the house consisted of two posts, between which was suspended the portrait of Oliver Cromwell, and it was often jocosely remarked that "Martin has hung the Protector." This old place has long since passed away, and the memory of the old house has perished from the present generation.

In 1740, David Ballou built a house that served as a tavern for many years, through the Revolution and beyond. Another tavern associated with the period was a house on present-day Main Street, purchased from Samuel Phillips in 1766 by Eliphalet Slack, who enlarged the building and turned it into a well-known hostelry. A long, hip-roofed edifice, with a continuous lean-to extending the line of the roof in the rear of the house nearly to the ground, was again a common American feature without English precedent.[6] The tavern is said to have entertained Washington and his officers on their way to Boston.

Outside of Providence Planations, as might be expected, taverns had a distinctly rural look and feel. The Benedict Arnold Tavern, built in 1693, was scarcely more than a simple wooden farmhouse, yet situated as it was in the township of Warwick on the northern end of Main Street between the Quaker Meetinghouse and the road to Providence, the tavern became a popular resort.

In a history of the town written in the late nineteenth century, Lieutenant Governor Greene of Warwick recalled that "the young people for many miles around in the long winter evenings were wont to assemble here and hold their merry makings."

As with other taverns, it was a gathering place for older members of the community as well to learn of the most recent news and events. The tavern had a long history, with the first license given to the widow Arnold and then passed to the son after her marriage to William Wenks. Benedict ran the tavern successfully and achieved a popularity that led him to become governor of Rhode Island. He was also the grandfather of the namesake who would become a general in the Continental army and disgrace the family name after being convicted as a traitor to the United States. The memories that Greene had of his nights at the tavern must have been especially wistful, as the old home was torn down in 1840.

Another old tavern in the vicinity stood on the old Apponaug Road, opposite the old "Fording road," before the building of the Pawtuxet River bridge in 1711. This establishment was at one time known as the "Warwick Hotel" and, by the late nineteenth century, had fallen into ruin and was reputed by locals to be haunted. On the corner of Post Road at what was known as "Apponaug Four Corners" stood the Apponaug Hotel and Puritan Candy Shop with its red striped awning. This view became a popular picture postcard at the hotel's gift store. Other growing communities would soon see taverns populate the main routes within Rhode Island.

Heading west from Providence, one of the earliest establishments the traveler encountered would have been the Mathewson House on Greenville Avenue. The gambrel-roofed house with its large central chimney was built in 1710 and expanded by the nineteenth century into a well-known hotel. With the expansion of the Hartford Pike, the Cornell family opened a tavern and hotel, which was later sold and became the Randall Hotel. This property was bought in the late 1800s by "Shang" Bailey, a one-time performer for the Barnum and Bailey Circus, whose stint as the "Shanghai Giant" no doubt led to the popularity of the hotel into the early twentieth century. Shang Bailey's tavern later found use as the Log Gift Shoppe, and the proprietors proudly displayed photographs and mementos of the past for visitors to enjoy. In 1976, the Ursillos, who were the current owners, applied for the old hotel to be placed on the National Register of Historic Places. That application provides us a glimpse into the early-nineteenth century hotel:

> The five fireplaces on the first floor have elaborate Colonial revival mantles with monochrome tile surrounds and hearths, as well as cast-iron fire boxes, which were installed c. 1896 by "Shang" Bailey. The eastern stairway, which is also a single flight, has an ogee-molded rail, massive turned newels and spindle balusters. The other woodwork in the eastern section includes a prominently molded chair-rail in the northeast and southeast rooms, more severely molded window frames and plain baseboards, all of which seem to date from 1833.

In 1733, Resolve Waterman built a tavern on the Putnam Pike, which is still a main road through the village of Greenville. As well as being an early stage stop in Smithfield, the tavern became a popular place for local gatherings, with a large dining hall on the first floor and a dance hall above. The tavern also housed an exchange during the village's formative years as rural farming gave way to industrialization and commerce.

Providence Journal photograph of the Resolve Waterman Tavern/Smithfield Exchange during restoration. *Courtesy of the Warwick Historical Society.*

The Mount Vernon Tavern, circa 1760. *Photo by author.*

The Brayton/Holden Tavern, circa 1697. Now called the Paine House, it is home to the Western Rhode Island Historical Society. *Photo by author.*

One of the town of Foster's earliest taverns served a similar purpose as the community around the house began to expand. What became known as the "Mount Vernon Tavern" was established in 1760 on the corner of Howard Hill road and the Plainfield Pike and was run by Benjamin Fry and Francis Fuller during its first years of existence. It was purchased by Pardon Holden in 1815 and, a decade later, held a bank within the western front room. For a time, the tavern became known as the "Bank House Tavern" but later reverted to the original name until it became a private residence in 1888.

The town of Coventry also held its share of taverns. In the Historical Register of the state's Historical Preservation and Heritage Commission, we find mention of the ruins of "a substantial Colonial tavern" that was situated on Sand Hill road and served as an overnight stop on the East Greenwich to Hartford stagecoach run.

Ordinaries and Houses of "Publick Entertainment"

Perhaps the first tavern, erected before the town was incorporated, was the salt box–shaped Brayton Tavern, built by Francis Brayton in 1748. The tavern keeper also owned a nearby mill and substantial landholdings. So much so, in fact, that the surrounding area was simply called "Braytontown" for many years. The tavern became known as the Holden Tavern by the nineteenth century, and it still stands today as the Paine House in the heart of Washington village and serves as the headquarters for the Western Rhode Island Historical Society.

In western Coventry, Samuel Rice built a two-story tavern with a central chimney in 1796 on the Great North Road, and legend has it that on opening night, at the stroke of midnight, he climbed to the roof, christened the tavern by smashing a bottle against the chimney and declared that all the surrounding area was to be named "Rice City," as it still is today. The tavern was long an overnight stop for the Providence to Norwich stagecoaches and was in business until 1866, when it was converted into a private residence by the local doctor and surgeon, P.K. Hutchinson.

Other nearby taverns flourished as well, including the McGregor Tavern, which had the distinction of becoming the only "temperance tavern" in 1831 and existed until it burned at the turn of the century. The Gibbs Tavern was built adjacent to Carbuncle Pond and existed until it, too, burned to the ground in 1924.

In the aforementioned village of Limerock, the Nathaniel Mowry Inn opened in 1817 and served as a relay house for coaches, being settled on the Post Road between Woonsocket and Providence. As such, Nate Mowry's house, with its expansive porch, large taproom and stable to provide fresh horses, accommodated a diverse group of clientele, and the proprietor proudly displayed a collection of drinking and dining ware from around the world.

A later tavern in the town would be built by Colonel Dexter Aldrich when he purchased the old Sheldon farm in 1822. The large, L-shaped house was named the Limerock Tavern, and it is said that the boundary line between North Providence (now Pawtucket) and Limerock ran through the center of the building. The locals came to call it the "Green Tavern" due to the shade with which Aldrich had originally painted the house. The front featured a wide veranda, and inside, the design was equally impressive:

> *Upon entering the front, a long reception hall extended the full depth of the house. The hall had fine paneled woodwork and an open carved staircase, leading to the upper floor. To the right were two large parlors while to the left, were two large rooms merged into one through a beautiful archway.*[7]

The signboard for the Nathaniel Mowry Tavern. *From* Stage-Coach and Tavern Days.

Aldrich's house also featured large fireplaces with intricately carved mantelpieces. By 1842, the role of tavern keeper was transferred to John Bishop and then to Benjamin Lindsey, who, though only managing the house for a few years, turned the place into a first-class establishment. The Lindsey Tavern came to have a nationwide reputation for its simple New England elegance. By 1850, Lindsey had passed on the tavern to Cyrus Hall and then to George Parish. When the house was purchased by Samuel Fales in 1858, he renamed it the Fales Hotel, though this was short-lived. When Fales sold the business to William B. Haile in 1870, the name Lindsey Tavern was restored. William Haile and his wife, Isabella, ran the tavern respectably into the 1880s, until tragedy struck and cast a long shadow over the tavern's remaining years.

A man named Henry Rush had become infatuated with the tavern keeper's wife and convinced Isabella to run away with him. Though she returned shortly after, the scandal and heartbreak devastated her husband, who was institutionalized in Providence's Butler Hospital. On May 31, 1882, Henry Bush returned to the Lindsey Tavern and, after a brief conversation with Isabella, shot her to death. When William learned of the crime, it further worsened his condition, and he died shortly after his wife at the age of thirty-five.

The Lindsey Tavern was bequeathed to the Hailes' fifteen-year-old daughter, Bernice. The child's grandmother, who had moved into the house, took on the role of tavern keeper, and Rebecca Comstock continued to run the place until Bernice's marriage to George Willoughby. The couple struggled to keep the tavern running, but upon her husband's death in 1917, Bernice closed the business.

As the years passed, Bernice continued to live in the old house, becoming somewhat of a recluse, sharing the rooms with dogs, cats and chickens rather than the elegant tea parties she had hosted in her youth. On December 15, 1943, fire ravaged the tavern, and Bernice Willoughby perished in the blaze at the age of seventy-five.[8]

Newport Taverns and Brewers

In Newport, one of the town's oldest houses became its first tavern. The massive home that Frances Brinley built for his family on Farewell and Marborough Streets was constructed in 1652. Twenty-one years later, it was sold to William Mayes and converted to a tavern. Mayes was an

The White Horse Tavern, circa 1652. *Photo by author.*

infamous pirate, preying on European vessels plying the Atlantic before his return to Newport. The British authorities fully expected him to be arrested upon his return and the booty he had taken confiscated, but instead he was welcomed back to the town and reputedly used some of his takings to purchase the house.

The White Horse Tavern soon became the meeting place for Rhode Island legislators much as the Mowry Tavern had in Providence a generation earlier.

The first mention of the tavern in travel journals that we find is from Dr. Alexander Hamilton, a medical doctor cum philosopher of Scottish descent who traveled along the eastern seaboard in 1744. *Gentleman's Progress: The Itineraium of Dr Alexander Hamilton* has been much quoted and treasured as a rare, unblemished glimpse of colonial life in the region.

On July 16, Hamilton arrived in Newport, "a pleasant, open spot of land, being an entire garden of farms." He writes of visiting the Market House and seeing the large Quaker meetinghouse and takes note of the churches in the vicinity, though his eye is also drawn to more secular attractions.

"This town is remarkable for pritty women as Albany is for ugly ones, many of whom one may see sitting in the shops in passing along the street. I dined att a tavern kept by one Nichols att the Sign of the White Horse where I had put up my horses."

Hamilton traveled on, visiting various towns in Massachusetts before turning back toward Rhode Island a little more than a month later:

> *I arrived in Bristol at one o'clock and a little after crossed the ferry to Rhode Island and dined at Burden's. I departed thence at o'clock but was obliged to stop twice before I got to Newport on account of rain. I went into a house for shelter where were several young girls, the daughters of the good woman of the house. They were as simple and awkward as sheep, and so wild that they would not appear in open view but kept peeping at me from behind doors, chests, and benches. The country people on this island, in generall, are very unpolished and rude.*[9]

The doctor and his hired man found their way into town by six o'clock that night, though the streets were enveloped in a thick fog, and with their bags, they were several times mistaken in the dark for peddlers by passing pedestrians. He returned to Nicholl's place at the Sign of the White Horse and would write that while "lying there that night, [he] was almost eat up alive with buggs."

Thirty-odd years later, when the Revolutionary War erupted, the proprietors fled the city rather than cater to the Hessians who had taken over the rooms of the house during Newport's occupation.

As early as 1700, Newport had become the commercial center of the colony. The city's first licensed brewer was David Sebre, who produced beer and ale until his death in 1745. George Rome and a group of Englishmen took title to a brew-house in exchange for a debt. The group successfully ran the brewery with Rome at the helm, until he returned to England at the outbreak of the Revolutionary War. His brewery was located on Spring Street, within hearing of the pealing bells of First Baptist Church. Other brewers and tavern keepers swelled the city by the sea, including John Lance, Anthony Young and Joseph Belcher.

Giles Hosier was an immensely popular brewer whose beer and ales were quaffed in taverns and houses within a wide area. The statehouse even rented him lagering space in the basement to help increase his production.

As with other colonial port towns, early Newport was awash with illegal dramshops, and authorities had to take drastic measures akin to the

Massachusetts policy, providing for a select group of men to "search out for all tippling houses and places that Entertain Slaves Servants or persons that reside or come into ye Town without leave of ye Town Council."[10]

In this manner, a number of unwanted and "illicit groggeries" were shut down. But with a harbor opened wide to world trade and the diverse crew members that such trafficking brought into the town, such houses doubtless remained amid the legal establishments that hosted the travelers who entered Newport by horse and carriage.

Production of rum was also of utmost importance, and twenty-one distilleries were operating on the island during the colonial period, when it was a hub of the "triangle trade," importing sugar and molasses from the West Indies and returning with rum to exchange for slaves sold right off the docks to farmers and wealthy Narragansett planters whose spacious farms extended on wide tracts of land from Newport into South Kingston.

KINGSTON INNS

The village of Kingston began its life known as "Little Rest," from the legend that troops marching from Connecticut and Massachusetts took a brief respite in town from their march to route the Narragansett Indians from the Great Swamp.

One of the first establishments for entertainment was the Tavern Hall Club. Built in 1738 by Elisha Reynolds, the tavern was also the site of the production of the county's first newspaper, the *Rhode Island Advocate*. Reynolds eventually sold the building to the Potter family, and additions were made to the old house, with the attic being converted into lodging rooms. In subsequent years, the tavern hosted students from the Kingston Academy, as well as operated as a grocery store.

In 1752, a large party of "gentlemen and others" from Little Rest petitioned the state's General Assembly for a new courthouse and jail to be built in the village, making the promise that they would offer "three good taverns well furnished and supplied for ye entertainment."

When the colony had been divided into counties in 1729, it was determined that the General Assembly, or the governing body of the state, would meet at locations in each county throughout the year. Since that ruling, the assembly had met at nearby Tower Hill.

The most popular tavern in the vicinity at that time was the house run by Squire Zimmanuel Case. The jovial tavern keeper was a friend of Benjamin

Postcard of the Kingston Inn. *Courtesy of the Providence Public Library.*

Franklin, who often stopped there during his tours of the mail run on the Post Road in his capacity as the King's postmaster for the colonies. At the height of the tavern's popularity, Case was known to inform his guests that his house was well known to "all gentleman travelers on the road from South Carolina to Piscataqua."[11]

Over time, the courthouse in Tower Hill fell into disrepair, the General Assembly continued to grow in order to represent the burgeoning population in the colony, and it became less desirable for legislators to meet there.

That same year, in 1752, Robert Potter opened a tavern on Main Street. Captain John Potter purchased land from Elisha Reynolds and built a tavern next to the courthouse site a few years later. Together, the taverns would host meetings of the South Kingston town council for many years. Captain Potter's house was known as the Baker Inn, the Babcock House and finally as the Kingston Inn. The tavern was long a stagecoach stop and also used as a gathering place for militia. Potter was an officer of the Kings County militia, rising to the rank of colonel in 1763.[12] A massive house with multiple fireplaces, it is still in use today as a bed-and-breakfast. Local legend recounts that while Washington did not sleep there, he took a respite from his travels in the tavern, long enough for a cool draft, before he and his party rode on.

In 1770, a sorely needed third tavern was finally built in Little Rest. As historian Christian McBurney writes, "when the General Assembly was in session, the Little Rest tavern keepers hosted the most important men from all over the colony. During General Assembly sessions, the taverns were so crowded that their guests sometimes had to sleep 'head to toe' in their beds."[13]

This third inn was opened by Thomas Potter Jr., who had a large house bequeathed to him by Elisha Reynods, his father-in-law. Potter called his establishment the "Sign of the Dove." As with other tavern keepers, Potter was occupied with state politics and ultimately served in the General Assembly for several terms. He also served in the local militia, reaching the rank of lieutenant colonel by the Revolutionary War. He served as host to Washington at Little Rest in 1781 and ran his inn until his own passing in 1793.

Robert Potter sold the tavern he had run to Thomas Peckham Jr. in 1796. Peckham continued to keep the old house in business until building a new tavern with a spacious drawing room and a bar for local patrons.

Another popular Little Rest establishment was the house that became known as the Joe Reynolds Tavern. The original proprietor was Caleb Westcott, originally a carpenter. Westcott sold the tavern to Joe Reynolds, who served as tavern keeper until his death in 1823, when the property was passed to his son.

Philip Kittredge Taylor wrote that the old house had under its roof at one time or another "almost every distinguished legislator, lawyer and public character who figured in Rhode Island's subsequent history."

One establishment built on the Post Road to accommodate travelers was the Willard Tavern, built by Willard Updyke in 1745, who gave the tavern its name but duly rented out the house to enterprising tavern keepers. Located on the border of the large plantation owned by Governor William H. Robinson, the house became a popular gathering place for the wealthy Narragansett planters who held many parties on its premises and dances in the long room on the second floor, which was entirely open space but for benches along the wall where the guests could rest between the lively waltzes.

The house was purchased by Stephen Wright in the early 1850s and remained in the family until the time that his great-granddaughters Mary Elizabeth and Mrs. Anna Gordon ran a popular tearoom there in the 1930s and 1940s.

I would be remiss if I did not mention, among these early taverns, the Philips Farm House in Wickford, which was at one time a tavern. Alice

Morse Earle describes the old house as having "a splendid chimney over twenty feet square. So much room does this occupy that there is no central staircase, and little winding stairs ascend at three corners of the house. On each chimney piece are hooks to hang firearms, and at one side curious little drawers are set for pipes and tobacco."

Such glimpses into these old houses give us insight into the early forming of community that these ordinaries and inns offered and the reason why they flourished so well in the first half of the eighteenth century. By 1749, the county of Providence had thirty-one licensed tavern keepers, and beyond the city, publick houses mushroomed along the main routes leading to other destinations. The reason for travel at this time was, of course, commerce. In the century from 1660 to 1760, New England underwent enormous growth in population, new townships and commerce. As early as 1660, population growth had led to the dispersal of people from the earliest settlements. By 1700, New England held about 120 towns. Sixty years later, the number of townships was nearly doubled, and during the early eighteenth century, many of these first townships became important commercial cities.

As trade expanded, outlying townships, which had long provided for themselves and their neighboring communities, became sources of goods for these expanding urban areas and beyond. Providence, like other port cities, literally had the world at its doorstep, and as demand increased, trade expanded in the inland communities from the lime kilns in Lincoln to the dairy farms in Smithfield and Johnston and the quarries in Cumberland. As historian Jack Greene has written:

> *Though the growing populations that inhabited New England's increasing number of urban places produced some of their own food and necessities, they all required significant supplements of both food and timber products. Together with the demand for those products for export to the West Indies and elsewhere, these requirements produced a lively commercial exchange between town and country, which were more and more linked by a proliferating network of roads, bridges, and ferries.*[14]

Although the Kings Highway from Boston to New York was a long maintained route and became the Post Road in 1693, the Providence-Norwich turnpike (Plainfield Pike) was not completed until 1714, and most of the major east–west roads were built in the early nineteenth century. These would include the Rhode Island and Connecticut turnpikes (Hartford

Drawing of Sarah Kemble Knight on horseback from *The Journal of Madam Knight.*

Pike) in 1803, the Powder Mill turnpike (Putnam Pike) in 1810 and the Foster-Scituate turnpike (Central Pike) in 1822.[15]

The maintenance of those increasingly used turnpikes and bridges became a growing concern. Likewise, so did the lodging available for those transporting goods and making other business transactions. Even as the economy and commerce were expanding, conditions of roads and the lodging and meals provided, in rural areas especially, remained widely diverse in character.

One remarkable account of the early varieties of lodging the traveler of this period could expect on the road is in the journal kept by Sarah Kemble Knight, who describes a journey that took her through "Narragansett Country" in 1704: "Being come to Mr. Havens' I was very civilly Received, and courteoussly entertained, in a clean, comfortable House, and the Good woman was very active in helping off my Riding clothes."

Having had some "Choklett" prepared in a brass kettle, Miss Knight writes that

> *I went to bed, which, tho' pretty hard, Yet neet and handsome. But I could get no sleep because of the clamor of some of the Town tope-ers in the next Room, Who were entred into a strong debate concerning ya Signifycation of the name of their Country, (viz.) Narragansett. One said it was so by ya Indians, because their grew a brier there of a*

prodigious Highth and bigness, the like hardly ever known, called by the Indians Narragansett; And quotes an Indian of so Barberous a name for his Author, that I could not write it. His Antagonist Replyed no—it was from a spring it had its name, wch hee well knew where it was, which was extreme cold in summer, and as Hott as could be imagined in the winter, which was much resorted too by the natives, and by them called Narragansett…and that was the originall of their places name—with a thousand Impertinances not worth notice, wch he utter'd with such a Roering voice and Thundering blows with the fist of wickedness on the Table, that it pierced my very head.

Despite this unfortunate evening, she left with the coach at four o'clock in the morning, setting out for Kingston with a French doctor for company. Miss Knight relates:

This Rode was poorly furnished with accommodations for Travellers, so that we were forced to ride 22 miles by the post's account, but neerer thirty by mine, before we could bait so much as our Horses, wch I exceedingly complained of. But the post encourag'd mee, by saying wee should be well accommodated anon at mr. Devil's a few miles further.

Lodgings there were no more suitable for Miss Knight, for among the pages of her scathing review is a poem, composed as she was in the habit of ridding herself of any undue irritant in verse. This particular composition begins: "May all that dread the cruel fiend of night keep on, and not at this curs't Mansion light."

On she continued to another ordinary where the "pretty full mouthed old creature" who conducted the house discussed her various ailments to the doctor in her company but paid scant attention to Miss Knight. From there she continued her journey, and "about one afternoon come to Paukataug River, which was about two hundred paces over, and now very high, and no way over to'ther side but this. I dared not venture to Ride thro, my courage at best in such cases but small, And now at the Lowest Ebb, by reason of my weary, very weary, hungry and uneasy Circumstances."

The doctor apparently rode on without her, and Miss Knight was forced to retire at "a little cottage just by the River, to wait the Waters falling." The proprietor promised to aid her safely across in "a little time," but the traveler dutifully recorded the cottage as *one of the wretchedest I ever saw a habitation for human creatures. It was supported with shores enclosed with Clapboards laid on lengthwise, and so much asunder, that the Light come throu' every where; the doore tyed on 'nch a cord in ye place of hinges, The floor the beare earth; no windows but such as the thin covering afforded, nor any furniture but a Bedd with a glass bottle hanging at ye head on't; an earthen cupp, a snall pewter Bason, a Bord with sticks to stand on, instead of a table, with a block or two in ye corner instead of chairs.*

To her great relief, Miss Knight resumed her journey to Stonington the following day. Just over seventy years later, a young traveler found that conditions remained much the same. Master William Rogers had journeyed from Philadelphia to Providence as the first enrolling student of the new Rhode Island College (now Brown University) then situated in Warren. His journal recounts the travails of his trip and the trials a traveler had to endure, even in the age of coaches and a comfortable chaise:

Thursday ye 30th (of April 1776)...At seven o'clock a.m. I left Providence with purpose of returning to Philada.—Danl. So kind as to take me in chaise in order to carry me to New London by land...we all din'd at little rest one Potters Tavern—far'd but poorly—no oats or hay for our horses—Roads for some part of ye Way past Description Bad—At sunset Danl. & myself got to Charlestown & put up at Mr Champlin's—a very good Inn...Charlst'n is forty-four [miles] from Providence. Very much fatigued tho' ye expectation of once more seeing my Dear Family raised in my Breast pleasing sensations.

The rigors of travel in Rhode Island must have been unsettling for the young man from the finely kept roads and highways around Philadelphia. By the turn of the nineteenth century, however, these rural byways and country lanes were becoming well traveled, and the need to maintain them held more importance for everyone from the rural farmer to the merchant on Main Street. Town budgets took on the responsibility of road repair and maintenance, sometimes raising money by lottery for a new bridge or using new technology in building macadam or "corduroy" roads in areas that traditionally washed out during winter.

Some taverns expanded and became inns along the coach roads. As this occurred, lodging became more reliable, and the old houses once dreaded for

Leveling A Road by Pavel Petrovich Svinin, circa 1812. The Russian visitor depicted numerous ordinary scenes like this one in his watercolor landscape. *From the book* Traveling Across North America 1812–1813, Watercolors by the Russian Diplomat Pavel Simin. *Harry N. Abrams Inc., New York, Khudozhnik Rsfsr, St. Petersburg 1992.*

their sparse lodging and poor meals gained a reputation as healthy respites from the rapidly industrializing urban areas. This kindled a nostalgia for the simplicity of life these taverns displayed, the honest labor and integrity of the tavern keeper and his family.

Two such establishments were the Arnold Houses, a stone's throw from each other in Smithfield, near the junction of Farnum Pike and what is now Church Road. Called "half-way houses" because they were approximately ten miles from Providence and an equal distance from Woonsocket or other destinations, they were the centers of bustling activity for more than 150 years. The older house, built around 1780, had an addition "with a separate outside door to the barroom, and a larger room for dances and gatherings upon the floor above."[16]

The house directly on Farnum Pike was then, as it is today, largely surrounded by fields and was run as a farm for many years. One of the few details that distinguish its use as an inn was the detail in the interior of the house. As described by Grover Jenks in an early *White Pine Series* monograph:

The interior of the second Angell House has a very delicately detailed stairway, and some very charming wood ornament and moulding in the

The Angell House, circa 1780, in Smithfield, Rhode Island. *Photo by author.*

principle downstairs room...The wall cupboard is out of the usual in the arrangement both of its doors, and the moulding and pilaster enframement; treatments that are very nearly echoed at the mantel.

These rural taverns especially, but even those within a short drive from a bustling urban scene, took on a romantic aspect that was to sustain them well past the days of horse and carriage and stagecoach, well into the era when country outings by automobile became a fashionable pastime. In the early nineteenth century, a Reverend Dwight wrote:

In a word, you found in these Inns the pleasures of an excellent private home. If you were sick you were nursed and befriended as in your own family...your bills were always equitable, calculated on what you ought to pay and not upon the scheme of gentlemen must which extortion might think proper.[17]

In the coming chapters, we'll learn more about these old ordinaries and houses of publick entertainment and their role both in how we formed our ideas of self-government and in the Revolutionary War. We'll learn how these old houses both reflected and shaped the culture of the unique colony of Rhode Island—often, in thinking and jurisprudence, an island unto itself. And we'll examine the lore and legends surrounding a few of these old houses, for many of them are still standing today, harboring a wealth of stories long-forgotten to our generation.

Chapter 2

WHAT WAS SERVED

Though taverns had been traditional establishments brought from the Old World to the new colonies in America, early settlers soon found that innovation was a necessity to produce the brews that had been staples of European diets for so long. In her book *Stage-Coach and Tavern Days*, Alice Morse Earle wrote that "in New England, drinking habits soon underwent a marked and speedy change. English grains did not thrive well those first years of settlement, and were costly to import, so New Englanders soon drifted from beer drinking to cider drinking."[18]

William Blackstone and John Eddington had been the first to plant apple orchards in the Bay Colony and then in Rhode Island when Blackstone moved to his secluded hillside fifty miles away, in what is now Cumberland. Within a matter of years, the fruit was being grown throughout the eastern colonies as far south as Virginia. Roger Williams wrote in 1660 to Connecticut governor John Winthrop that his letter "was as welcome as a cup of your Connecticut cider." He was not long in waiting before cider became the most produced beverage in the colony.

A resident close to the Sayles Tavern and farm remembered the apple and pear orchard that grew in the triangular plot between Pidge Lane, Williams Road and the Post Road. Taverns throughout the colony did the same, turning wasted barley fields into orchards and pressing cider to sell in local markets and to travelers in the taverns. Though not native to Rhode Island or the other colonies, "the American climate was perfect for Apple trees…New England's cold, crisp weather was ideal…Production of hard

An early colonial pewter tankard from Newport, circa 1700. *Rhode Island School of Design Museum.*

cider expanded rapidly as orchards matured. For some regions, apples became the undisputed crop of choice."[19]

By the 1720s, production had become so widespread that a village of only forty families was able to press and ferment three thousand barrels of hard cider in one season. Cider was served at breakfast, lunch and dinner, used in cooking baked ham or even chicken. According to New England lore, new mothers in colonial times even nursed their babies on cider.

What was drunk in the taverns, of course, depended also upon the purse of the traveler. Each tavern along a main route between New England cities would have kept a collection of imported liquors to serve the wealthier clientele, if so inclined by delays or conversation. If the tavern keeper was not brewing beer, he bought from a local brewer and likely pressed cider and fermented homemade apple brandy. In the burgeoning years before the American Revolution, Newport was flush with vineyards providing local wines to communities throughout the colony.

EARLY HOME BREWING

The brewing of beer, as we have seen, also had a strong tradition in Rhode Island by the eighteenth century. In fact, beer and ale, though beset by the lack of good hops and malt in those early years, were still the drink of choice for many who could afford the luxury. Local brewers who imported their ingredients from European countries produced a steady supply once established, but home brewing took a decidedly American turn, especially in the rural areas beyond Providence and Newport. As such, the homemade beer and ales served varied from tavern to tavern.

An early historian of colonial times noted that "the poorer sort brew their beer with molasses and bran, with Indian corn malted with drying

A colonial kitchen in the James Arnold House. *Courtesy of the Warwick Historical Society.*

in a stone: with persimmons dried in a cake and baked; with potatoes with the green stalks of Indian corn cut small and bruised, with pompions, with Jerusalem artichoke which some people plant purposefully for that use, but this is the least esteemed."

Alice Morse Earle noted that Rhode Islanders preferred a brew made with pumpkins and molasses. They were in good company. Washington was said to have favored a brew with molasses, something similar to what we today would call a stout, and like today's bottled, handcrafted brews, no two were alike.

In Providence, Rhode Island, in the 1720s, Major Thomas Fenner, who would in time command all the land-based militia in the colony, opened a tavern near Neutaconkanut on the western edge of the city along the old route that ran through Scituate and then into Connecticut. Fenner's home brew became widely prized throughout the region, not only in his tavern but also in others, as he sent barrels to Warwick and Newport from his family's wharf on the Providence River, a block below the Sabin Tavern. Fortunately for us, among his legacy as a justice of the peace, a storekeeper and a surveyor, Fenner also left the recipe for his home-brewed ale:

> one ounce of sentry suckery or solindine one handful red sage or large 1/4 poundshells of iron bruised fine take ten quarts of water steepit away to seven and a quart of molasses wheat brand baked hard one quart of malt one handful sweet balm take it as soon as it is worked.[20]

An immensely popular drink in this early period was "flip," a beer-based beverage that held a wide variety of ingredients. In *Stage-Coach and Tavern Days*, we find the recipe for this uniquely American beverage:

> Flip was made in a great pewter mug or earthen pitcher filled two thirds full of strong beer, sweetened with sugar, molasses, or dried pumpkin, according to individual taste or capabilities; and flavored with "a dash" —about a gill—of New England rum. Into this mixture was thrust and stirred a red hot loggerhead, made of iron and shaped like a poker, as the seething iron made the liquid foam and bubble and mantle high and gave it a burndt, bitter taste so dearly loved.

Another recipe for the drink instructs the tavern keeper: "in a quart mug break three eggs…add three teaspoons sugar and stir well…add in a jigger of rum and a jigger of brandy, beating meanwhile. Fill remaining volume of mug with beer…insert red-hot iron until it hisses and foams."

WINE, CORDIALS AND COBBLERS

Sack, or wine, was also widely drunk in the colonial tavern. The drink was named for the strong, dry wines of the sherry variety that came mainly from Spain, Portugal and the Canary Islands. By the eighteenth century, the name applied to any sweet wine, even from local vineyards. Sack was used in the making of sack-posset, a traditional drink used to toast the married couple at weddings, and even in Puritan times, it was drunk with a psalm and a prayer.[21]

By far, the most-consumed beverage by the common traveler was "punch," which, like other beverages, varied widely, often being a concoction of an innumerable combination of spirits. One old recipe from a tavern in Pawtuxet Village demonstrates a decidedly strong version called "Fish House Punch":

> *Dissolve ¾ pound of sugar in punch bowl…Add a bottle of lemon juice… add two bottles of Jamaican rum…one bottle of cognac…two bottles of water…one wine (glass) of peach cordial….put a big cake of ice in the punch bowl…Let punch stand about two hours.*

In addition, "small drinks," or lesser beverages, were also served. Cocktails such as cobblers, toddies and grog were commonly drunk. Champagne and sherry cobblers gained popularity in the hot months of summer. Served with cracked ice that frosted the glass and garnished with fruit, a local saying was that the drink was as "refreshing as an east wind." In comparison, toddies were the choice for the traveler frozen from rough roads and ice storms in the age of travel on horseback and coaches. A hot beverage liberally laced with rum and sugar, it warmed the hands and stomach of many a stranger by the hearthside.

Grog, a beverage generally of rum distilled with water, could also mean any diluted cordial and soon became the byword of any cheap beverage and those who imbibed them. In Providence in the late 1700s, along what is now called South Main Street, stood a group of derelict old houses named derisively by the wealthier neighbors as "rotten row." These held grog houses and rooms that housed, among others, a man named Prout who made the rounds of nearby taverns with his trained bear.

Other drinks served varied from "ciderkin," a watered-down hard cider, to simple vinegar water, hailed as a refreshing beverage from the times of Roman soldiery.

A silver cup from the collection of the Codddington family. *Rhode Island School of Design Museum.*

THE SERVING TABLE

Just as beverages varied from tavern to tavern, so too did the fare that was offered. In many cases, towns and villages set a fixed price for meals and lodging to keep a continuity for consumers who, in rural areas, often had to travel miles before the next establishment. In some cases, tavern keepers were required to distinguish between a "good meal" and a common one. Meals often cost more than the lodging, especially if the lodging included sharing a bed with a stranger or companion. One example from the Bowen Inn of Barrington tallies the bill for Mr. and Mrs. John Tripp during their stay in May 1776:

> *To 1 dinner...........................9*
> *To bread and cheese................. 7*
> *To breakfast and dinner.......... 1 3*
> *To 1 bowl Toddy..................... 9*
> *To lodging you and wife........... 6*
> *To 1½ bowl of toddy......... 1 1½*
> *To 1 Gill Brandy................... 5½*
> *To breakfast.........................9½*
> *Mug Cyder....................... 1½*
> *To ½ bowl Toddy................. 4½*
> *Dinner............................. 8*
> *To 15 Lb tobacco at 6d.............7 6*
> *To ¼ bowl Toddy...................4½*
> *To ½ Mug Cyder................. 1½*
> *To Supper............................6*

It is interesting to note the difference in shillings between "dinner" and what we must assume was a less extravagant meal for "supper." Large meals were often scheduled around the time of stagecoach arrivals. One English traveler lamented the practice, writing that "at each house there are regular hours for breakfast, dinner and supper, and if a traveler arrives somewhat before the appointed time for any one of these, it is in vain to call for a separate meal for himself; he must wait patiently for the appointed hour, and then sit down with the other guests that may happen to be in the house."

Most often, taverns served what they could procure from their own farm or local markets. For rural taverns, this meant that fare was often simple:

similar or the same as what the family running the house served themselves. This, of course, also depended on the season. The summer travelers might find themselves served a local favorite of "Green Corn Pudding," the ears of corn scored before the kernels were cut to let the sweet "milk" flavor the dish. The fall season might produce a plate of "red-flannel hash," a concoction of assorted diced, cooked meats stewed with potatoes, cabbage, turnip, carrots and garlic vinegar. A colonial housewife might have brought a copy of Hannah Glasse's *Art of Cookery Made Plain & Simple* and used another New England staple to make her recipe for "A Ragoo of Onions":

> *Take a pint of little young Onions, peel them, and take four large ones, peal them, and cut them very small; put a Quarter of a Pound of good Butter into a Stew-pan, when it is melted and done making a Noise, throw in your Onions, and fry them till they begin to look a little brown; then shake in a little Flour, and shake them round till they are thick; throw in a little Salt, and a little beaten Pepper, and a Quarter of a Pint of good Gravy, and a Tea Spoonful of Mustard. Stir all together, and when it is well tasted, and of a good Thickness, pour into your Dish, and garnish it with fry'd Crumbs of Bread or Raspings. They make a pretty little Dish, and are very good. You may strew fine Raspings in the room of Flour, if you please.*

As historian John Larkin notes:

> *Country taverns were organized like large households, and tavern cooking was home cooking, spanning the entire range of rural New England roadways. Its quality varied greatly, just as it does in homes and restaurants today. Where the tavern keeper was stingy or the cook unskilled, the food could be awful...At some taverns, the fare was good but amazingly simple. In smaller and more remote communities, breakfast and supper sometimes reverted to the most frugal and traditional patterns of the New England diet: fried cornmeal or "rye and Indian" bread crumbled into milk.*

Travelers to Rhode Island's harbor-side communities could expect a wide variety of chowders and casserole-like dishes made from what the Portuguese sailors who frequented Fox Point in Providence would call *frutti de mare*, or "fruits of the sea"; an expression so long in use that it came to denote any seafood platter or casserole served up off the wharves. In Pawtuxet Village's Gaspee Archives, we find a number of old handwritten recipes from the popular taverns there. They include meals of "Haddock chowder" and "Yankee Codfish with Gravy." One particular old recipe for "Hasty Pudding" proved to be useful for serving multiple times during the course of the day. The original recipe reads as follows:

> *Put two quarts of water into a clean dinner pot or saucepan, cover it and let it become boiling hot over the fire; then add a teaspoon of salt, take off the light scum from the top, have secured to use some sweet fresh yellow or white corn meal. Take a handful of the meal with the left hand, and a pounding stick in the right, then with the stick stir the water around and by degrees let fall the meal; when one handful is exhausted, refill it; continue to stir and add meal until it is as thick as you can stir easily, or until the stick will stand in it; stir it awhile longer; let the fire be gentle; when it is sufficiently cooked, which will be in half an hour, it will bubble or puff up; turn it into a deep basin. This is good eaten cold or hot, with milk or with butter and syrup or sugar, or with meat and gravy, the same as potatoes or rice.*

The author notes that, in the village, this was a particularly favored meal for Sunday night suppers served "with stripped salt codfish on the side." In rural areas, this staple was often served as supper on its own. Writing to his wife before retiring for the evening, one traveler wrote: "my hominy [corn meal mush] and milk supper will do now to sleep upon."

Breakfast in New England was, as traveler Samuel Goodrich noted, "no evanescent thing" and often included "ham, beef, sausages, pork, bread, butter, boiled potatoes, pies, coffee and cider." Rhode Island establishments in Little Compton, Kingston and Narragansett served up the local favorite called "jonnycakes" with butter and maple syrup. Another staple made from cornmeal, the flatbread recipe is derived from its Native American origins and was first called "Jonakin," though the name, and recipe itself, took on several Anglicized versions. One prominent Rhode Islander named Thomas Robinson Hazard even published a book extolling the staple. From his *Jonny Cake Papers*, we find a description of the family cook at the hearth:

> *Phillis, after taking from the chest her modicum of meal, proceeded to bolt it through her finest sieve, reserving the first teacupful for the special purpose of powedering fish before being fried. After sifting the meal, she proceeded to carefully knead it in a wooden tray, having first scalded it with boiling water, and added sufficient fluid, sometimes new milk, at other times pure water, to make it a proper consistency. It was then placed on a jonny-cake*

Interior of the Kings Arms Tavern, Newport. *Photo by author with the kind permission of Mrs. Natalie King.*

board about three-quarters of an inch in thickness, and well dressed on the surface with rich sweet cream to keep it from blistering when placed before the fire. The cake was next placed upright on the hearth before a bright, green hardwood fire supported by a heart-shaped flat-iron... When the jonny cake was sufficiently done on the first side, a knife was passed between it and the board, and it was dextrously turned and anointed, as before, with sweet, golden-tinged cream, previous to being again placed before the fire.

In the cities of Providence and Newport, more lavish dining was to be found. Those establishments of the more well-heeled variety served sumptuous suppers and an astonishing variety of desserts. Menus were handwritten, and patrons perusing them could expect to find mock-turtle soup, oyster patties, boiled bluefish with oyster sauce, boiled chickens with oyster sauce, corned beef and cabbage, roast beef, lamb, chicken, veal, pork and roast turkey, to name just a few entrees. Dessert might be any assortment of fruit pies—apple, peach and berry in season, as well as pumpkin, squash and mince pies in the fall. Custards and puddings were also popular desserts.

By the beginning of the nineteenth century, with stagecoach travel increasing and bringing passengers over long distances, hearty meals could be found in the outlying taverns. In the Pawtuxet taverns, one could dine on roast venison, mulligan stew or mutton, among other fare. Of course, if you were traveling by stagecoach, you often had little time to relax and enjoy the meal, as one traveler attested:

> *At Providence coaches were ready: on flew through the dust and sweat of the day like Jehus. At the tavern dinner was ready, but there was no contract for time to eat; after Grace from Dr. Cox (too long for the occasion) we began to eat. Scarcely had I swallowed half my first course when in came driver hallowing "all ready." I thought there was a stable-yard understanding between him and the landlord, for while we were brushing the dust from our clothes, mustering and saying grace, he was eating and drinking as fast as he could, and I did not observe that he paid anything.*[22]

GAMES, GAMBLING AND OTHER DIVERSIONS

With such diverse travelers sharing beds, the dinner table and one another's company in what were generally small dwellings, one might wonder what those grouped together did to entertain each other or what the tavern keeper might provide by way of entertainment.

Many travelers, like Miss Knight, wrote disparagingly of the inns and "hovels" they found, but others, more seasoned to the rigors of the road and perhaps more open to adventure, looked forward to the gatherings in the crowded, boisterous taprooms that they would encounter, and they relished the opportunity for home cooking beyond their own region of culinary experience. They too, as Lafayette, noted the importance of these taverns as a gathering place of communal respect and equality. As Sharon Salinger notes, "Taverns offered colonists one of the few sources of secular division and amusement in early America. Locals or travelers could attend scholarly lectures, listen to musical entertainment, or gaze upon unusual animals."[23]

Like drinking itself, games, shows and a variety of forms of entertainment had long been part of tavern culture in Europe. Puritan leaders in New England were determined to repress such entertainment in their communities. To this end, such houses that permitted dice and billiards, as well as cards or any games that had strong affiliations with gambling, were often severely penalized along with the gamblers involved. Nonetheless, as

The Lindsey Tavern, Limerock/Fairlawn. *Courtesy of the Johnson Research file at Pawtucket Public Library.*

taverns and public houses grew in more secularized communities, games such as backgammon, bagatelle and especially cards came into wide popularity. These games were legal in the taprooms of most colonies as long as money was not being wagered. One old reminiscence of an early Providence establishment is a likely example of others throughout the region:

> *In the house opposite the foot of Bank street Martin Seamans kept a tavern accommodating much traveling customers and not a little from the town. A pretty numerous number of grave and revered seignors assembled there two or three evenings in a week to partake of supper and a game of cards.*

Often a customer would "get picked" and lose badly to these locals. The proprietor would purportedly commiserate with his losses as he headed for the door, while cheerfully encouraging him to return, as his luck would surely change, since this was, after all, "a money-making place."[24]

In rural Rhode Island, horse races were held in the fields used for training militia. In Narragansett, they were held on the beach. As those who frequented the taverns were often conscripted in the militia in the towns, wrestling and boxing matches were common. Turkey shoots and sharpshooting also found a place for friendly competition on tavern grounds.

Postcard of Market Square. *From the author's collection.*

The Kings Arms Tavern, circa 1696. *Photo by author.*

What Was Served

One of the early edicts issued by Providence Plantations in 1647 determined that "every person from the age of seventeen years to the age of seventy" was to own a bow and a minimum of four arrows. The notion of the council was that it was "both more man-like and more profitable" to practice archery when assembled than to indulge in other sports and games of chance.

Music and dancing were staples of tavern life from the moment people opened their homes to travelers. As we have seen, Rhode Islanders were freer than the other colonies in seventeenth-century law. Massachusetts and Connecticut, for example, lumped traveling performers of all kinds with beggars, rogues and itinerant preachers, calling them "vagabonds" and providing that they should be whipped, fined and either removed to a place of settlement or expelled from the colony.

Dancing, in particular, drew large crowds of people to Providence as well as to houses in rural areas, where couples arrived by lamp-lit horse and carriages at houses teeming with light, laughter and frivolity.

While visiting among the more prominent families of Providence in the summer of 1788, Susan Lear wrote in her journal that she "rose this morning after a sleepless night as we were kept awake until after three o'clock listening to the music in the neighborhood."

Unfortunately for Miss Lear, John Brown's house where she was staying was easily within earshot of the Sabin Tavern and even the Olney Tavern in Market Square, if a raucous enough crowd had gathered.

The Greenville Tavern sported a large dining hall with a dance hall above, off of which was a long, elevated porch for private walks. The Western Inn in Burriville, a well-known stagecoach rendezvous, was well known for its diners' gregarious appetites in the taproom and the pounding of boots on the dance floor above. The Anthony Aborn Tavern in Pawtuxet was equally famed for its dinners and dance hall. The Golden Ball Inn on the Post Road featured a long, canopied driveway where the well-dressed suitors could disembark from the coaches under shelter and enter the long ballroom of the house. The Lindsey Tavern, at the crossroads of Limerock and Fairlawn, featured a large ballroom on the second story whose wide planked floor "appropriately bounced" and seemingly lifted the dancers from one step to the next.

So popular was the pastime that even the smallest of houses held dances—the aforementioned Benedict Arnold Tavern would be but one example.

Newport, by some contrast, offered a more highbrow variety of entertainment. In June 1762, a handbill was passed around the city advertising that on Monday, June 10, the Public Room of the Kings Arms Tavern would host

A Series of Moral Dialogue in five parts
Depicting the evil effects of jealousy and other bad passions and Proving
that happiness can only spring from the pursuit of Virtue.

Despite these lofty offerings in the tavern, the crowds were likely better for the dancing that took place on Thursday nights, when gentlemen could "spend the evening" for twenty-five cents.[25]

More formal musical consorts were often held in the taverns by the sea, and most popular of all were the private lotteries. These were the only licensed form of gambling in Rhode Island and other colonies and became wildly popular in every community. Nearly every aspect of the community participated in such lotteries, from churches and social groups to the communities themselves when roadwork, building schools or new civic establishments were promoted. Towns and villages often used lotteries to assuage public debt. Such gambling was staunchly justified by officials: "The interests of literature and learning were supported, the arts and sciences were encouraged, religion was extended, the wastes of war were repaired, inundation prevented, travel increased, and the burden of taxes was lessened by lotteries."

MINSTREL SHOWS, CIRCUSES AND SIDESHOWS

By the early 1800s, the New England colonies were in the midst of a dire economy, and this certainly accounted for a loosening of the laws and the consent from Massachusetts in 1805 and Rhode Island in 1813 to allow towns and villages to collect license fees for entertainment at their discretion. A generation later, Providence was one of the most popular minstrel towns in the country, with circuses, variety combinations and minstrel shows originating tours from the city. It was during these years of traveling shows and circuses that a famous incident occurred in the village of Chepachet.

In 1822, a broadside was circulated in the village announcing the impending arrival of the "Fabulous Learned Elephant," a twelve-year-old pachyderm recently acquired by the veteran showman Hakaliah Bailey. The six-thousand-pound elephant, affectionately called "Little Bett" by

Old postcard of the Chepachet Inn. *Courtesy of the Providence Public Library.*

her admirers, was the latest of several elephants that Bailey had trained to perform counting and spelling tricks for appreciative audiences around the East Coast. On July 31, the keeper and her guards brought the docile beast into town under cover of darkness, erecting an enormous tent behind the Chepachet Inn where the price of twelve and a half cents granted an adult admission to see her perform. Children were charged half price. For many in the town who had never seen an Indian elephant before, Little Bett was a wonder to behold. She entertained the crowds for nearly a week before Bailey and company traveled on.

In the spring of 1826, Bailey and "Little Bett" returned, again setting up a tent behind the inn where, no doubt, the showman expected a great reception. On this visit, however, fate was to take an unkind turn for the trained pachyderm. According to local historian Evelyn Kent, a group of boys from the village snuck under the tent, avoiding the price of admission, and were roundly kicked out by the guards. Intent on revenge of a kind, they later snuck back to the tent while Bailey and his helpers entertained themselves in the tavern and took his prized act for a walk. They got as far as the bridge above the Chepachet River, where the frightened animal refused to budge, and in anger, the boys shot her with their muskets.

Such a senseless act weighed heavily on the village's conscience for many years. On the 150th anniversary of Little Bett's death, the town placed a commemorative plaque on the bridge where the crime had taken place, and the Rhode Island General Assembly declared May 25, 1976, to be "Elephant Day," and the citizens have commemorated the event ever since. The bridge itself, though long replaced by other spans since the events of that spring night, is now known throughout the village as Elephant Bridge.

Chapter 3

MURDER AND THE
MOWRY TAVERN

As we have seen in our first chapter, the Mowry Tavern, being the first designated tavern in Providence, was a place of council meetings and religious worship, along with its everyday existence as a place of lodging and entertainment. The tavern was to have a long history, existing in some form or another until the turn of the twentieth century, when the old building was taken down. But despite that long history, the Mowry Tavern was to become associated and most remembered for a dark crime committed within sight of its door and the one instance when it was made to serve as a jail.

Until the winter of 1660, young John Clawson[26] must have considered himself a fortunate man. He was found by Roger Williams with some natives in a "lost naked and starving condicion." The founder of Providence Plantations took Clawson into his own home, where "I was not only his Master, (and he my house hold servant by ye year) but his school (master) giving him my Dutch testament and spending much time to teach him to reade."[27]

He grew to manhood and prospered, becoming a proprietor in the lands of Providence and one of those called "the five-and-twenty-acre men" for the land use rights they held.

Clawson and others held rights to a large swath of land, recorded as "all the lands between the river of Pawtucket and the river of Pawtuxet." He is listed in town records as a carpenter, and an inventory of his tools shows that he must have held considerable skill in that craft.[28]

Above: Nineteenth-century photograph of the Mowry Tavern from Mary C. Crawford's *Little Pilgrimages Among Old New England Inns*. Photo by *James Allen*.

Opposite: Map of early Providence settlements as shown in *Early Houses of Rhode Island*. Photo by *James Allen*.

But whatever fortune and happiness had been afforded young Clawson, all that was to change after an evening of drink and conversation at the Mowry Tavern.

On the early morning of January 5, 1660, the carpenter's prostrate form was found on the path leading away from the corner across the Towne Road where the tavern was situated, along a desolate area known as a burial ground and bordered by clumps of barberry bushes.

Clawson's face and chest had been brutally bludgeoned with a broad axe, and he was taken in a dying and delirious state to the nearby home of his benefactor. There, during the hours of suffering that passed, he was tended to by Benjamin Herndon and his wife, who "gave him sack and sugar whilst he lay wounded." The dying man was surrounded by friends, and both Williams and his wife tended to his bedside, along with the nurse "Goode" Wickenden

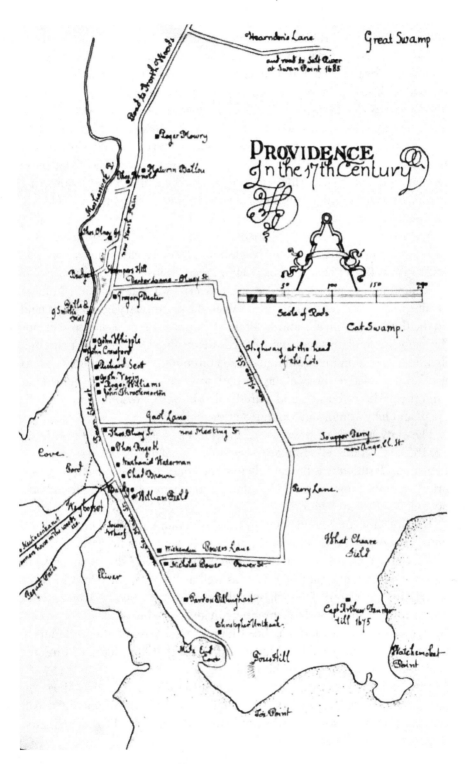

and one Mistress Throckmorton. During this time, despite the difficulty in speaking caused by his wounds, he purportedly accused Herndon of being responsible for the assault and cursed his children and grandchildren "to be marked with split chins and haunted by barberry bushes."

As much as these may seem to be the ravings of a delirious and desperate man, those gathered around Clawson knew the gravity of his accusation. This was, in fact, the first murder that had occurred in the Providence. Despite the dying man's accusation, suspicions among town officials fell upon "Waumanitt,"[29] a Native American known locally as an itinerant "wandering Indian" who took odd jobs from local farmers and town merchants. He was apprehended and taken to the Mowry Tavern.

As Providence had no implements as such for the imprisonment of a citizen, the town quickly enlisted blacksmith Henry Fowler, who was paid six shillings and three pence for irons to bind the prisoner.

Waumanitt was heavily guarded at the tavern by a hastily mustered militia of nine men for two and a half days. When the preliminary hearing was held on the third day, Williams and Valentine Whitman served as interpreters for the native defendant's testimony. It was determined for the court through their interpretation that Waumanitt had committed the act. Lying in wait as his victim strolled leisurely along the path toward home, he had stepped out from the barberry bushes, and with the first blow, "Clawson's chin was split open, and he was mortally wounded in the chest."

The early records of the town of Providence simply state that on March 12, 1660, "the Indian (Waumian) plead guilty of killing John Clawson—then Benjamin Herndon was brought before the court in suspition that he was a principle in the murder…said Herndon plead not guilty…the jury found him not guilty and cleared him."[30]

The town meeting voted "that the prisoner Waumanitt shall be sent down unto Newport to the Collony prison there to be kept until his tyme of triall."

A longboat was found, and the two men escorting the prisoner were provisioned with one pint of liquor, as well as "powder and shott to carry along with ye prisoner." Much speculation has risen over the years as to whether the longboat and the three ever made it the thirty miles to Newport. No record of a trial there has been found, only those of the preliminary hearing in Providence. Alice Morse Earl writes that "the Indian Murderer vanishes down the bay out of history."

Tradition tells us that many in town continued to believe that Herndon had a hand in the murder, possibly that he had hired Waumanitt to kill Clawson, but no reason as to why these two early settlers in Providence came to this fatal impasse has ever been discovered. A look at the court records in the years before the murder, however, give a glimpse into the character of Benjamin Herndon and perhaps the reason his townsmen suspected his actions. They also suggest a possible motive and may, in fact, implicate him and his wife in an attempted coverup after the crime.

Herndon was not a man without scandal before he moved to Providence. He was taken to court in Lynn, Massachusetts, in December 1647 on the charge of beating his wife, an act witnessed by Ezekial Gilbert and Henry Collins. His wife was also taken to court some years later, accused of stealing clothing from Mary Pray.

In Providence, Herndon seems to have routinely argued with his neighbors. He was served a ten-pound bond in February 1659 to appear in court on March 2 to answer to the "breach of peace and fright committed on the family of William White." On August 31 of the same year, he was brought to court by Samuel Bennet "because he suffered great damage in his corne" from the defendant's swine.

In the years that followed Clawson's murder, Herndon's brushes with the law continued, leading to him being brought to Newport in 1667 charged with "assaulting, resistancing with force and voyolence the constable in the execution of his office."

In October of that same year, he brought charges against "William Harris, Thomas Harris Sr. and Thomas Harris Jr.," who had entered his property "and did there with force and armes assault Herndon."

Though many of his townspeople carried their suspicions for years after the crime, Roger Williams seems not to have believed in Herndon's involvement. In March 1, 1671, we find recorded in the Providence records "noated by ye Towne that ye deed which Roger Williams hath this day presented betwixt Benjamin Hernton and him selfe, as a deed of sale upon John Clawson's house and lott recorded in our Towne Booke verbaton."

Herndon records the price for the house and lands at eleven pounds five to be paid to Roger Williams in the first year, three pounds the second and "the third year following in cloth and stockings and corne, and aples at he common and usual price." The early records of Providence shows that Herndon paid his debt early, for on March 11, 1674, we find: "Roger Williams records six shillings and nine pence which makes up the full sum of eleven pounds for which Roger Williams sold Benjamin Herndon the house and land that was John Clawson's."

One might think that this would raise suspicion ever higher, but there is no record beyond the legal fights and occasional physical skirmishes that any further investigation occurred during Herndon's lifetime. There are a few curious factors that we can raise today and examine.

In October 1659, John Clawson had sold rights to some of the lands he held to one Richard Prey (Pray), except for the lot adjacent to Benjamin Herndon's. This in itself was not unusual, as the early records of Providence contain many sales of lands, even exchanges among the growing settlement, but one wonders if this lot was purposefully kept to avoid Herndon expanding his own holdings.

Why was Clawson brought to Roger Williams's house, a distance of some one and a half miles from the scene, rather than a closer dwelling or even the Mowry Tavern? And by what means? Given the man's wounds, even a wagon ride must have been excruciating.

In his dying hours, Clawson had implicated Herndon in the attack. Elizabeth and Benjamin Herndon, by their testimony, had been the first to administer aid to Clawson at Williams's house, raising the suspicion that the "sack and sugar" administered to the gravely wounded man might have been not so much for comfort as an attempt to keep the talkative patient inebriated and perhaps perceived as in deliriums. Williams later wrote that "he spake by fits and could not answere a word to many questions."

I have found no records, scarce they be for this whole affair, to implicate that there existed any dispute over land or land rights use before the murder, though Roger Williams refers to some "goods" of the victim that may have been in others hands at the time of Clawson's death. As Williams wrote, "it is possible [that] lying so still he might muse of his and desire [that] I might helpe him to get them out of other mens hands."

Benjamin and Elizabeth Herndon, in effect, persuaded Roger Williams that John Clawson would have wanted his benefactor to inherit his estate though refuted that claim in court later. Williams, writing in his defense as the caretaker of the estate, wrote that "in ye afternoon when Elizabeth Herndon upon his asking again for me, asked him whether he meant [that] his Master should have his goods: her words sound, and others say and mine Eares told me from her own Relation [that] she thus understood him as I did."

Williams offered that "it is far more probable [that] lying by ye Graves mouth and going into his Coffin (of which he spake) and being put in mind to dispose of his Goods, I say it is more rationall to thinck he so minded than to quarrel upon Law many years before ended."[31]

It may seem odd that Williams was forced to defend himself in taking hold of an estate that belonged to a man he had supported nearly his whole life. Williams wrote to the court that "I had vever pennyworth of his, but

Portrait of Roger Williams from his *The Bloody Tenent of Persecution*, London, 1644. *Courtesy of the John Carter Brown Library at Brown University.*

spent much time and charges about his business and grieved at his Folly and Frowardness, and gave him all possible Helpe and Favour."

The town had taken the young Clawson to be a runaway apprentice, and surely the greed and zealotry for choice parcels of property that had plagued

Today, a cement walk covers the path Clawson took that fateful night. *Photo by author.*

Providence's founder for some time by 1660 would have included the holdings of a young man many likely felt was undeserved to be a freeholder. These sentiments may have spilled out on occasion within the tavern, for Williams also wrote that "Ed(ward) Inman testifies [that] he hath heard John Clawson complaine of other men as Roger Mawrie [Mowry] Sam(uel) Bennet Mr Arnold (to whom he writ for him but never of myself)."

Eventually, the elder Williams retained control of the late Dutchman's estate, selling a large part of that parcel of land to Ephiriam Pray and then two twenty-five-acre parcels to Thomas Olney and John Field. He then sold the parcel, along with the house that Clawson had built with his own hands, to the man who most held responsible for his murder. One can only surmise that without Williams as his benefactor, Herndon and his family would likely have left Providence long before his death in 1686.

And what of Waumanitt and the men who had left with him for Newport? Could they have simply vanished as part of a greater plan to gain Clawson's holdings? Even in 1660, it would gave been an easy matter to take a bribe in one colony and slip away to another or to almost any part of the world from the "city by the sea."

But that is only speculation, which is all one can offer, based on the tenor of the times.

A century after the murder, the story of "The Curse of Clawson" was written in popular and dramatic style by the Honorable Theodore Foster, who compiled an account of the murder and trial along with the more current observation that "the descendants of the murderer were remarkable for the excavated or furrowed chin which causes the curse of Clawson to be kept in remembrance." Foster compiled a compendium throughout his adult life of curious stories, histories and odd facts, and early historians combing through the former senator's papers discovered the tale and have used it in their own narratives of the Mowry Tavern history.

Edward Field wrote in his memorable *Colonial Taverns* that for years after the crime, the place remained "a lonely, dark and grewsome spot, and it is related that travelers along the road always whipped up their horses or walked at a more rapid gait, when they reached this place and called to mind the dark deed there committed and the curse of Clawson."[32]

On June 10, 1700, the town council, in considering "some convenient parcel of land…to lie in common continuality to be for the use of military affairs for training of soldiers and ctr; and also to be for the use of burying the dead," chose that forlorn place of common land leading back to the Moshassuck River, adjacent to the trail where John Clawson had been mortally wounded.

Chapter 4

RHODE ISLAND TAVERNS IN
THE AMERICAN REVOLUTION

By the dawn of the American Revolution, European nations looked askance at the rogue colony across the Atlantic, certain that these revolutionaries in New England had made their mad claims to liberty in a moment of drunken fervor. "The Americans are madmen," fumed one German newspaper, "running about under the sun with a torch in hand, searching for daylight…And what of us? What is one to think of…ale-house politicians, who favor the cause of the Revolution, who seem to grant a certain warmth to the fate of the colonials?"[33]

At the time, though the outcome was unexpected, the scribe could not know how close he had writ his assertion. Edward Fields, in his *History of Providence Plantations*, writes of the role of taverns in early New England:

> *The tavern was the center around which the whole town swung. The townsmen assembled within its spacious rooms on town meeting day; the town council here held its sessions; notices for the information of the people were posted upon the tavern door, and the traveler from a distant town found here refreshment and shelter. The traveler was always a welcome guest for the news and gossip which he brought.*

It was a place, as well, that any man could speak freely, and as dissension with the Crown's policies began to grow, the tavern rooms filled with sometimes heated but healthy debate as the yeomen, merchant sailors, farmers and small businessmen aired their grievances and declared what

Undated drawing of the Olney Tavern and the Liberty Tree. *Courtesy of the Rhode Island Historical Society.*

freedoms should be righteously regained or preserved in the colonies. The Sons of Liberty in Providence, born as in other New England cities after Great Britain's imposition of the Stamp Act, dedicated a great elm outside of Captain Joseph Olney's tavern to be "a tree of liberty." According to the *Providence Gazette,* "An animated discourse was delivered from the summer house in the tree, by a son of liberty" that Monday afternoon in July 1768, "after which formed the ceremony of dedication."

Thus, Rhode Islanders, as the other colonies of New England, fomented their designs on liberty for a decade before the Declaration of Independence was writ in Philadelphia, but it was the actions of a small army of these patriots that would ultimately lead other Sons of Liberty and the united colonies to the cusp of that independence.

THE SABIN TAVERN

On the evening of June 9, 1772, the Sabin Tavern, like others around Providence Plantations, was seething with "people drinking drams of flip, carousing and swearing." The Sabin was a "double wooden framed house of two stories" resting at the foot of Planet Street, a stone's throw from Fenner's wharf along the Providence River. The location made it a popular hostelry for stevedores and ordinary seamen as the wharf was the docking place of a regular packet ship between Providence and Newport, as well as a fleet of smaller boats bringing wares and goods to local markets.

Nineteenth-century photograph of the Sabin Tavern from Mary C. Crawford's *Little Pilgrimages Among Old New England Inns. Photo by James Allen.*

As darkness fell on the waterfront, news came in the form of a crier, beating a drum and calling out that the hated British patrol ship the HMS *Gaspee* had run aground at Namquid Point. Sailors knew this meant that the ship lay helpless until the early tide, well after midnight.

The *Gaspee*, under command of Lieutenant William Dudingston, had been haunting the waters of Narragansett Bay for some months, overhauling all manner of vessels, even small boats bound for market, and occasionally plundering a local farm on shore.

The Bowen house on Benefit Street in Providence, where young Ephraim took his father's rifle to the Sabin Tavern a block below. *Photo by author.*

In March of that year, the *Providence Gazette* had informed its readers that "a number of men belonging to the armed schooner that has been for some time past cruising in the river interrupting the traders, firing on Oyster boats and we are told landed on the Narragansett shore a few days since and carried off several Hogs belonging to the inhabitants, and also a Quantity of firewood."[34]

That morning, the *Gaspee* had pursued the sloop *Hannah*, on the bay from Newport, certain of taxable cargo hidden aboard. The *Hannah*'s owner, merchant John Brown of Providence, was among the first informed of the British ship's vulnerability. According to the account published in Bartlett's *Records of the Colony of Rhode Island*, Brown immediately "directed one of his trusted shipmasters to collect eight of the largest boats in the harbor, with five oars to each; to have the oars and row-locks well muffled, to prevent noise, and to place them at Fenner's Wharf."

Within hours, the tavern was a hive of activity, and an oral account years after the event, from Ephraim Bowen, gives us a glimpse into the hours preceding the burning of the HMS *Gaspee*.

Rhode Island Taverns in the American Revolution

About nine o'clock, I took my Father's gun, and my powder horn and bullets and went to Mr Sabin's, and found the south-east room full of people, where I loaded my gun, and all remained there till about ten o'clock, some casting bullets in the kitchen, and others making arrangements for departure, when orders were given to cross the street to Fenner's Wharf, and embark.

Under cover of darkness, about sixty men, Captain Abe Whipple and John Hopkins among them, slipped out to the wharf. The men were divided into the eight boats with a captain appointed to each and Brown overseeing the operation. The small flotilla pushed off and rowed toward the point where the *Gaspee* lay aground.

In the hours ahead, as dawn slowly began to rise in the east, those on the dockside peering through spyglasses and binoculars toward the distant Namquid Point would have seen the flames erupting that would soon engulf the British vessel.

According to later accounts, John Brown was the last to leave the burning ship, determined that no one should leave with any scrap of evidence that might lead to identifying the men who had taken part in the raid. Indeed, those who were interviewed later were resolutely united in professing their ignorance of the entire affair.

Of course, Providence knew better. According to some written histories, there were many on hand to see the Sons of Liberty off to the stricken ship, and many of those were relatives who would hear the events of that night recounted many times in the years following the Revolutionary War.

The lore associated with this historic event and the tavern itself would grow in the coming years and lead to a strange odyssey from what were modest beginnings. The early history of the tavern, as given in an address by the historian Edward Field, tells us that the house had originally been the home of Captain Woodbury Morris, who purchased land in 1757 and built the house shortly after. Seven years later, Morris died on the coast of Africa. His widow, Mary Morris, continued to live in the house, and by her account, Mr. James Sabin was living there by December 1765 and "catered to the wants of man and beast."

The tavern Sabin operated on the first floor of the house would bear his name and lend itself to the historic house, even after he had left in December 1773, with land of his own and a new tavern near Market Square.

The property was then bought in 1785 by Welcome Arnold, who had built his own massive house just above the tavern on Planet Street five years before. Arnold made several additions to the building, and

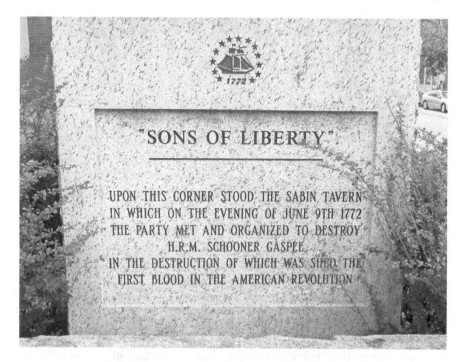

The Welcome Arnold House, circa 1780, on Sabin Street, Providence. *Photo by author.*

he enshrined the Gaspee Room into a formal dining hall with Ephraim Bowen's account written in longhand by his daughter, framed above the mantel.

Welcome Arnold died in 1798, passing ownership of the old tavern to his eldest son, Samuel Greene Arnold, who then passed the house on to his younger brother, Richard James Arnold, who used the house as his residence.

During his ownership, Richard Arnold added an "ell of brick to the house with an entrance through an archway into the 'Gaspee Room.' A good many years afterward, he built a third story to the house and put an octagonal end on the famous southern room."[35] This is the formidable structure that appears in colored postcards and early photographs.

After this remodeling was completed, the house became known locally as the Gaspee House and hosted addresses and meetings of local historical societies for many years. With Richard Arnold's death in 1873, the famous house was passed on to his two sons, whose interest in keeping the property soon waned, and "the historic dwelling was taken over by the Providence Institute for Savings."[36]

By 1889, the house was in dire disrepair. The bank held the house with the intent of finding a suitable purchaser, but it was finally sold at auction to W.R. Talbot, the husband of Richard Arnold's youngest daughter. Talbot had purchased only the house in auction, and his efforts to negotiate a lot for the massive building all failed. By 1891, the house was slated to be demolished, but Talbot took all pains to save the Gaspee Room. As recorded by a pamphlet printed in 1931:

> *It was detached very carefully from the rest of the structure, along with the adjoining portion of the hallway and even the staircase itself. Placed on rollers as one unit, it was moved up and over the crest of the hill to Mr. Talbot's own home at 209 Williams Street. This was just as carefully attached to the Talbot house, becoming an integral part of the latter. All the wainscoting and paneling from the original hallway had been studiously saved and was used over again. A new chimney had to be built, but it was put together out of the old brick of the old chimney, and the same square tiles and hearth were used. The mantel above the fireplace was reconstructed out of the timbers from the kitchen of the old house, in which the patriots had molded bullets. Upon this mantel were cut inscriptions which told the history and significance of this room.*

In January 1892, Mrs. Talbot organized the Gaspee Charter of the Daughters of the American Revolution (DAR) in the famous room, and with her oversight, the charter was able to purchase the house in December 1929, with the dedication of its new home on January 12, 1931. The Daughters of the American Revolution held the house until 1975, by which time the organization's membership had declined, and the Talbot house was given to the Rhode Island Historical Society (RIHS). Today, the Gaspee Room remains intact, though again in private hands. The RIHS sold the house in 1983 to a private buyer who turned the house into condominiums. Few passing by the curious address of 209A Williams Street know the history of the quaint room affixed to one end of the large nineteenth-century manor. One has to notice the bronze plaque affixed by the doorway and strain to read the history of the room seen in ghostly stillness through the glass.

As the conflict with Great Britain grew to be inevitable, local militias were quickly formed, made up from eligible men in the district, and drills were conducted either on fields adjacent or in nearby community taverns, as free ale was the salary paid to recruits when the marching was done. As early as November 1638, the council of Portsmouth declared the twelfth of

Postcard of the Gaspee House, circa 1869. *Courtesy of the Providence Public Library.*

Addition of the Gaspee Room, as seen today. *Photo by author.*

November as "a general day of Trayning for the Exercise of those who are able to beare arms in the arte of military discipline."[37] Able-bodied men between the ages of sixteen and fifty years of age were expected to attend, and most did, not just for the ale, but as a display of civic unity and self-governance that was an early characteristic of the colony. In succeeding fashion, later towns and villages followed suit.

LOCAL MILITIAS AND "TRAYNEING DAYS"

Throughout the colony, towns established parade grounds and training days. Taverns were often the focal point of these gatherings as well as historical events through the years of Revolution and the young republic that followed. In Rhode Island, traditional training grounds and those taverns associated with training days were pressed into service for recruitment and muster. These included the Peleg Arnold Tavern in Unionville, on the coach road between Providence and Woonsocket, and the Battey Tavern in Pawtuxet, which according to historian Edward Bittel "stood at the Post Road edge of a large, open field which the Pawtuxet Artillery used as a training ground for many of its musters." Horace Belcher would later note that these "trayneing days" were also an opportunity for the community to set up root beer stands and sell other refreshment to the large crowds that gathered to watch the drills.

The Kentish Guard began its drills in a field adjacent to the Bunch of Grapes, the tavern built by the popular merchant William Arnold on North Main street in East Greenwich. So esteemed was the tavern that when fire destroyed the Arnold House in 1788, a petition was circulated among his neighbors to help with the expense of rebuilding. William and his son Stephen operated the newly constructed hotel for many years. The building still functions as a pub today, and guard members still gather for a pint on the anniversary of the militia's founding.

In Providence, this would culminate with the use of the wide expanse known as "Jefferson Plains," the gentle slope and wide field where the classically designed marble statehouse was built in 1900. In one of a series of lectures given in Providence in the first half of the nineteenth century, former mayor Walter R. Danforth recalled that the Plains

furnished a retired promenade for all classes of citizens, and was much frequented for its extensive prospect and salubrious air. It was then the

The Peleg Arnold Tavern.

*place for general muster for the militia at a regimental or brigade review…
the review ground was unbroken save by the Fenner-Angell tavern, and
that on such occasions was used as a sort of barracks, for their officers
and soldiers; and citizens there found a supply of solid condiments and
liquid stimulants.*[38]

These taverns and others throughout the colony were to become familiar
to regiments that remained to train, recruit and patrol, often marching
through the day from one tavern to another. A young sergeant named John
Smith, serving in Captain Loring Peck's company from Bristol, became a
diligent diarist of the average soldier's maneuvers, marches, skirmishes and
sometimes desperate foraging along the eastern seaboard communities in
the closing months of 1776.

Smith's journal, and others, as we shall see later, reveal that the routine
of a soldier was far less romantic than those who had sent their sons and
husbands into the revolution might have imagined. Setting out from Bristol
on an early March evening, the troops languished for hours on a breezeless
bay—"we were out almost all night on the water," Smith wrote. The
company finally put in at South Ferry around three o'clock in the morning
and immediately dispatched Ensign Joseph Read to purchase rum at a
nearby tavern. The crew was found out, however, by one Colonel Hoxie

and ordered to abandon their casks and head on to Newport and Fort Liberty. The boys from Bristol duly boarded the boat and were forced to row against wind and tide to the fort, where they were promptly punished upon landing.

After ten days at the fort, the company received orders to proceed to New York. Having become all too painfully familiar with the stringent rules at the fort, Smith and company might have expected those rules to be somewhat lax away from the watchful eyes of superior officers, but they soon found that they were sadly mistaken. Smith wrote:

> *As soon as the sun arose the fifteenth day of September, we proceeded on our march for John Potters Esq. where we were to Loge this night. Capt. Peck had the Command of this Division in all four Companies he going ahead forbidding the tavern keepers from seling any Liquor to the Soldiers without an order from An officer which Caused some uneasiness Amongst the Soldiers Belonging to his Division.*[39]

Despite this setback, Smith recorded that he "sleept well this night in a Good feather Bed in Potters house whilst the Regt. Slept on the floors in his Entrys and under the Baggage Carts and Elsewhere out of doors."

Sometimes, a tavern owner, already a self-established leader in any community, became one in the ranks and on the battlefield as well.

Major Simeon Thayer returned to Providence after serving with other Rhode Island troops in Benedict Arnold's expedition to Quebec in 1775. He built a large house at the summit of Constitution Hill and named it the Montgomery Tavern after his beloved commanding officer. The signboard that hung above the tavern door is said to have borne the likeness of the distinguished general.[40]

Benjamin Arnold of Warwick, Rhode Island, was the proprietor of the Golden Ball Tavern, a large house he had built in 1760. The tavern, or inn, as it was sometimes called, had already been a long-standing stagecoach stop before the coming of the Revolutionary War. Arnold and his son both served in the Continental army at much personal loss.

Early in the conflict, Arnold's sloop, the *Sally*, had been captured by the British—no small loss for a tavern supplied with sack from Newport's vineyards, as well as an array of imported "strong liquers." The senior Arnold served as captain of the Pawtuxet Rangers, the militia that oversaw the defense of Warwick from Pawtuxet Neck and took part in the Battle of Rhode Island. His son would march with other Rhode Islanders through

The Golden Ball Tavern, later purchased in the nineteenth century and known as Cole's Farm for many years, until its demolition in 1951. *Courtesy of the Warwick Historical Society.*

muddy lanes and into fields of battle in New Jersey, as well as Brandywine and Ticonderoga, in New York.

The Golden Ball became the scene of many an after-muster gathering and spirited debate as news arrived with messengers on horseback of the outcomes of battles and troop movements far away. On occasion, throughout the war, history would be made in one of these old hostelries.

THE DAVID ARNOLD TAVERN

One such tavern was the David Arnold Tavern, located on the "Main road in Old Warwick, a few rods south from the road to Warwick Neck." Arnold's brother Caleb also kept a public house in the town, and both establishments were used for town meetings throughout the Revolutionary War. Because of its proximity to the newly constructed Fort Neck, as well as its spacious lawn, the David Arnold Tavern was the site of militia drills accompanied by fife and drum in its march to the fort.

Rhode Island Taverns in the American Revolution

Rhode Island had, with the events in Boston in 1775 and the bombardment of Bristol in November of that year, responded by quickly regrouping local militias, appointing officers to the regiments of the "Colony's Brigade" and preparing for war. In the spring of 1776, the *Report of the Committee appointed by the General Assembly, relative to the Military Defences of the Colony* recommended that

> *one company, be placed at Point Judith; one company, at Boston Neck, between Narrow River and the South Ferry; one company, at Quanset Point, in North Kingston; one company, at Pojack Point, in North Kingston; and Potowomut Neck, in Warwick; one company, at Warwick Neck; half a company, at Pawtuxet, in Cranston; one company at Barrington; two companies at Bristol; one company, at Bristol Ferry, on Rhode Island side; and one-third of said company, on Tiverton side; one company, in Tiverton and Little Compton, near Fogland Ferry; four companies and a half, on the island of Jamestown; and the remainder of the troops, being seven companies, together also with the artillery company, at headquarters, on Rhode Island.*

But an even greater number of Rhode Island recruits were sent elsewhere to join battles in Quebec, then New York and New Jersey as the war heightened. As historians Robert Bray and Paul Bushnell point out, "Rhode Island never seemed to have enough soldiers. To be sure, the center of the war was far away…but its reality was brought home almost daily to the Rhode Islanders through the incursions of British raiding ships into towns all along the shoreline of Narragansett Bay."

The assault and then capture of Newport in December 1776 must have surely cast a pall as dark as the winter skies over the colony. To the soldiers dug in at forts or bivouacked in smoky camps while their officers met and drank in the nearby taverns, the consequences of their bold declaration must have surely come to light, yet for many in these ranks, this only increased their determination to turn the tide against Great Britain. One such officer was assigned to the Tiverton regiment under Colonel Benjamin Stanton, on an outpost that now bears his name.

Major William Barton was from Warren and, having also served in Newport, knew the waters of Narragansett Bay very well. After the defeat of Newport and the capture of his friend General Lee, the major was soon devising a plan that was sure to be a blow to the British troops carousing so freely in the harbor city.

Barton had learned that the British general Prescott was suddenly paying frequent visits to a house about five miles above Newport on the west road

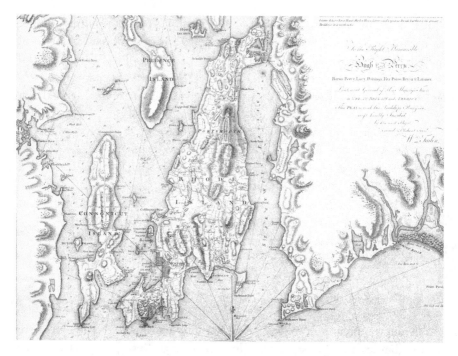

Map of lower Narragansett Bay from Blaskowitz's *Map of Narragansett Bay,* circa 1777. *Courtesy of the John Carter Brown Library at Brown University.*

to the Bristol Ferry. The house belonged to the widow Overton, whose attractions had led the general to a lapse in judgment, as he frequently spent the night in her company with but one sentry posted outside.

An escaped soldier from Newport named Coffin confirmed this to the major, along with details of the house itself. This information allowed Barton to solidify his plan and present it to Colonel Stanton. The colonel reviewed the plan and issued an order on July 5 for Barton to take forty-one volunteers and "attack the British army."

The major's plan was simple yet unpredictable and, as Barton knew, unexpected to the British mindset of conducting war. In effect, Barton and several boatloads of soldiers would row across Narragansett Bay under cover of darkness and take the British general prisoner. The major quickly assembled troops and went directly to Warwick Neck, where they would set off. The weather delayed them a day, and then another, and it was only there, likely in the tavern with draughts of rum to fortify their courage, that Barton told the volunteers of their bold mission to come.

It was only in knowing Narragansett Bay so well that Barton could have developed his plan. By rowing between Patience and Prudence Islands, the five boats under his command eluded the British guard.

Upon landing, one man was left in each boat while the other troops quickly made their way to the widow's house. The lone sentry was easily overtaken and held to silence at gunpoint, while the men entered the house. The general was found upstairs and taken prisoner in his nightclothes. A Major Barrington, the general's aide-de-camp who had been sleeping in an adjacent room, was captured when he leapt from the second-story window. The prisoners were quickly hastened to the boats, and the general, with only an overcoat thrown over his nightgown, was placed in the boat with Barton. The men set off again and rowed back as quietly as they had come, unnoticed by the British vessels anchored off Hope Island. They "coasted the west shore of Prudence, passed around the southern end, and arrived in Rhode Island" just a little over six hours after they had departed.

Upon returning to Warwick Neck, the general was procured a pair of shoes after much protest on his part that he should march even a short distance without them. A soldier who had accompanied the expedition was sent to find a pair at the nearby fort, and this accomplished, the prisoners were marched to the David Arnold Tavern, given rooms and held overnight.

After breakfast the next morning, they were delivered to Providence by carriage under armed guard. From there, the general was transported to Washington's headquarters in New Jersey. As Barton had hoped, the British released General Lee in exchange for Prescott the following spring.

OTHER TAVERNS IN THE WAR

In the fall of 1777, the Pawtuxet Artillery, after the surrender of the British at Saratoga, would escort a number of General Burgoyne's troops along the familiar route through Connecticut into Rhode Island, on their way to Boston, where the prisoners of war had been promised safe passage home.

Marching along Post Road above Pawtuxet, they had paused at another popular house, known as the Carder Tavern, which became host to a brief reunion with families and neighbors of the troops before they moved on to Providence.

Throughout Rhode Island, troops continued to muster and to recruit for the anticipated battle against the British in Newport. Those who had

The Carder Tavern. *Photo by author.*

enlisted marched for days between Providence and the outlying villages of Rhode Island, gradually increasing their ranks as the summer came, and marching recruits back to barracks at University Hall. One such soldier was Jeremiah Greenman.

The young man had enlisted in Providence at seventeen, been sent with troops to Quebec, was taken prisoner and went AWOL on release. He reenlisted in Coventry under Shaw and General Nathanael Greene in February 1778. By May, his regiment was marching and recruiting constantly, as well as drilling new soldiers for the coming campaign.

On May 7, Greenman wrote: "This day about 12 o'clock lift Providence with the wagons / pushed as far as Cranston where we oated our horses / then pushed on as far as Furniss woods where our wagon got sat."

Greenman rode on horseback and led the regiment to Waterman's Tavern, where they waited for the wagons to arrive. The troops spent the night in nearby woods and the next morning woke to "rain and cule / hired a pair of oxen to get our wagons / we pushed on as far as watermans tavern where we

The Waterman Tavern, circa 1747. *Photo by author.*

Undated photo of a family outside the Sayles Tavern. *Courtesy of the Johnson research files, Pawtucket Public Library.*

got our wagons mended and continued all day in Coventry / thirteen and six pence for board."

The Waterman Tavern, built in 1747, had long been a popular stop off the Great North Road. During the Revolutionary War, incidents like the one Greenman describes would have been common. The tavern was the scene of town meetings, political elections and military planning. The stories from these gatherings would only be enhanced later in the war, with the arrival of the French commanders Rochambeau and Lafayette on their way to Yorktown in June 1781.

Rochambeau's army had left Providence over a succession of days, so that the tavern saw a staggered parade of infantry, wagon trains and artillery brigades arriving well into the night. In all, 5,500 troops were encamped in adjoining fields around the tavern and across the old turnpike.

In the tavern itself, the young Lafayette is said to have angrily swung his sword at an aide, only to have the saber lodge in the wooden mantle above the fireplace The mark from Lafayette's sword can still be seen today.

The Marquis de Lafayette was to leave his legacy with a number of taverns in the region. This teenaged nobleman had sailed from Paris in the early summer of 1777 to seek a commission as an officer in the Continental army. By this time, the Congress had witnessed a parade of Frenchmen seeking to become high-ranking officers, but Lafayette managed to impress Washington, and by the season's end, he was with the commander as well as General Greene, spying on the British from Grey's Hill above the Chesapeake, as the redcoats came ashore.

In early August 1778, Lafayette arrived "outside of Providence" with two thousand troops gathered from Washington's army, including the Rhode Island regiment under command of Colonel Israel Angell. The French fleet, due in no small part to Lafayette's influence, had finally arrived off Newport, and now troops were mustering in preparation for the Battle of Rhode Island. Lafayette spent the night in the Jeremiah Sayles Tavern while his troops encamped in pastures a fourth of a mile north of the old tavern.

THE SAYLES TAVERN

What was now the Sayles Tavern had begun as the Ox Tavern as early as 1641 and was situated at the junction of the Post Road and the Connecticut Turnpike. The tavern operated a toll at the intersection and had a large barn for passengers and stagecoaches to refresh their horses nearby. By the time of Lafayette's first visit, the tavern had been doubled in size, with the original stone end replaced by a massive central chimney that supplied a fireplace to every room in the house. With spacious sleeping quarters upstairs, the tavern on the first floor provided ample entertainment and provisions, as well as much-anticipated news and information. Due to its location, the tavern was a regular stop between Boston and Providence, a route that saw an increasing number of coaches and mail packets.

The Sayles Tavern had been the scene of an earlier celebratory event at the beginning of the Revolutionary War. In April 1776, Washington had marched his troops along the Post Road, where he was welcomed at the tavern by a large crowd, including the local infantry, and from there escorted by two regiments of Rhode Islanders under command of General Nathanael Greene to the governor's house in Providence.

Lafayette's first visit to Sayles Tavern was brief. He followed General Greene with his half of their combined troops a day later, where they gathered in Tiverton with great expectations for an American victory. But a series of events was to undo the marquis's expectations and the hoped-for acclaim for himself and his fellow countrymen.

General John Sullivan of New Hampshire had been appointed commander of the American assault. The plan was for the soldiers of the Continental army to cross the Sakonnet River and invade the eastern side of the island, while four thousand French marines, already waiting at Jamestown, would come from the west. These actions would, of course, be supported by an extended bombardment of the British fortifications from the French fleet in the harbor.

Despite what seemed like a solid plan, there were difficulties from the start. The French admiral D'Estaing was insulted by the makeshift camps of soldiers onshore and disappointed that they numbered only ten thousand men. The French fleet itself had arrived only after a long and arduous journey, and many of the seamen noted by Greene and Lafayette as they boarded ships for councils seemed hardly fit for a prolonged battle. Commander Sullivan completed ferrying his troops and their horses and cannon to Portsmouth but delayed the attack on the morning of August 9, though by noon of that same day, the war had come to him.

By 1:30 p.m., it had become clear that the sails on the horizon that Lafayette and others had been watching for more than an hour were a fleet of British ships from Howe's command in New York. The Rhode Islanders on shore felt a pall cast over their hopes for a quick and decisive victory. The French quickly withdrew their troops from Jamestown and eased away from

A portrait of the Marquis de Lafayette. Paris, 1783(?). *Courtesy of the John Carter Brown Library at Brown University.*

Prise de Possession de L'Isle de Rhode-Island en Amerique, par les Anglois, en December 1776. Courtesy of the John Carter Brown Library at Brown University.

the harbor. The British flotilla continued until 5:00 p.m., when thirty-five large ships lay anchored between Point Judith and Beavertail Light.

The French eased further away while the British lay in harbor, and both fleets were soon caught in a sudden gale that lashed at the sails and toppled masts while the boats were pitched furiously for two days. The troops on shore were soon hunkered down, sitting out the wind and rain as best they could, lined along the labyrinth of stone walls that crossed Portsmouth's fields.

D'Estaing soon informed Sullivan that his ships were too battered to commit to battle and would make their way to Boston for repairs. Despite appeals from Greene and Sullivan, the French left the scene and, to Lafayette's disdain, were subject to a scathing letter from the American generals that questioned the honor of the admiral and his actions that were "highly injurious to the alliance between the two nations."

American soldiers were also leaving the scene. By August 28, Greene told Washington that the troops were down to between "four and five thousand," a loss he found "truly mortifying."

In the end, the much-anticipated Battle of Rhode Island has been portrayed by most historians as little more than the brief salvos of cannon fire that each side exchanged and the pitched skirmishes that occurred on the island.

Lafayette was bitterly disappointed. He had ridden hard to Boston in an effort to convince D'Estaing to return, but the battle was over before his return. The British would not leave Newport until October 1779, when they abandoned the city in an effort to support the faltering campaigns in the south.

Two years after the Rhode Island campaign, Lafayette found himself again at the Sayles Tavern. In the intervening years, he had returned to France and helped to solidify support for the American cause, a part Washington urged him to play in smoothing ruffled feathers from the unfortunate beginnings of the alliance in Rhode Island. By the summer of 1780, the British had departed Newport, and the French commander Marshal de Rochambeau had encamped with his troops on the island, sending part of his expeditionary force to join Lafayette in camps above Dexter House. Lafayette was to spend several weeks in the tavern, impatiently writing to Rochambeau in mid-August that the French brigade should join Washington as soon as possible:

> *If you knew how strongly England and the Tories endeavor to persuade the Americans that France only wishes to kindle, without extinguishing the flame...I will confide to you that thus placed in a foreign country, my self-love is wounded by seeing the French blockaded in Rhode Island, and the pain I feel induces me to wish the operations to commence.*

Rochambeau's response was brusque. He had no desire to leave Newport to what he was sure would be a swift recapture of the city and the humiliation of the French brigade he would be indebted to leave behind. Washington was also reluctant to enact Lafayette's plan of action. In his letters, Rochambeau often deferred the marquis' ambitious plans to insist that he wait for word from Washington. The missives between the young American-appointed commander and the elder French general grew nearly as heated as the sweltering summer that passed that year. At one point, Lafayette wrote in exasperation to the general, "It is pointless to detail these plans minutely, and since you approve of assistance of this kind, I shall tell you frankly that we are wasting precious time and that military preparations should have begun already."

Eventually, the exchanges cooled, with Rochambeau giving affectionate and fatherly advice to the now twenty-one-year-old commander, urging him to retain "a coolness of judgment in the council room" as Lafayette set out for his long-awaited meeting with Washington in Hartford on September 20.

On the march to Hartford, Lafayette and his troops rested at the Angell Tavern in Scituate. The tavern had been built in 1710 by Captain Thomas Angell on a parcel of land that included a stretch of the nearby Ponagansett River. As with other taverns, the Angell House had held town meetings for years until the building of the Baptist church. The earliest mention of the tavern during the war is found in Greenman's diary. In July 1778, the young soldier's regiment was on the march to the anticipated battle in Newport. On July 31, Greenman wrote:

> *this morn started from Vallington / proceeded on our route as far as Coventry about 18 miles from providence ware we grounded our arms / it began to wrain / we took up our arms and put them in a shed /about 4 oClock we peraded marcht 6 milds to Scituate to angels tavern ware we pitched our tents and was order'd to wash all our Cloaths and clean our arms.*

On this occasion, according to local historians:

> *Lafayette encamped his regiment on the pleasant intervale in front of the house…*[he] *lodged in the tavern, and another French officer of high rank and accommodations in a house nearby, where lived Mr. Abel Angell. Mr Angell's wife…used to speak of making porridge for this officer, whom she called General, while he was sick at her house.*

This was certainly Rochambeau, who accompanied Lafayette to the meeting with Washington but must have fallen ill a day or so after leaving Newport. Despite the delay, or perhaps because of it, the troops met by the locals seemed in good spirits. They spent time bathing in the river and washed clothes to dry on tents in the sun. One resident, reminiscing at the turn of the nineteenth century, remembered that "the old people used to speak often to their children about the fine music of the band, as in the morning and evening they played in the camp."

Lafayette and Rochambeau would return from Hartford and wait for Washington's orders. The young marquis would later fight with distinction and earn his reputation in the South before eventually joining Washington and Rochambeau at Yorktown.

Those soldiers long-encamped near Sayles Tavern would be sent off to rendezvous with the remainder of Rochambeau's men, and during that great battle in June 1781, a French soldier writing at the time remembered the women pressing food into their hands as they passed, and they marveled at the plentiful goods, having spent a year or more in the poorly fed camps.

It must have been a lively scene, and the diary and drawings of Jean Batiste Antoine de Verger give us a whimsical portrait of the diversity of the soldiers and costumes that made up the French brigades. In many cases, our own American troops were very similar in appearance, as local regiments fashioned their own uniforms for war.

Rochambeau returned to greet another contingent of French troops in 1782, arriving in Providence around noon on November 10, marching two brigades up the Old Boston Post Road and encamping in a wooded area opposite the Old Dexter House. When the owner objected to the general's plan to deforest the area and build a barracks, the troops marched north again until reaching the old campgrounds used by the French under Lafayette. The road that led uphill to these pastures now bears the French commander's name.

Rochambeau stayed in Providence, but the officers of the French fusiliers repaired to the tavern, leaving a record of having paid the owner, Jeremiah Sayles, the sum of forty-three dollars and thirty-four pence for "four cords of wood at two dollars per cord, fences destroyed, &c."

Lafayette was to visit Sayles Tavern again during his extended tour of the nation, arriving on August 23, 1824, by carriage from Plainfield, Connecticut, and being met at the tavern by "a great military and civic procession. The ovation extended him was fully equal to that of Washington...and was participated in by the veterans of the Revolution, and by their children and grandchildren."

It was on this occasion that Abigail Pidge, daughter of Jeremiah Sayles, having married Ira Pidge, who now owned the tavern, and given birth just days before to a yet-unnamed infant, was inspired and asked the aging general for his blessing to name her son for their distinguished visitor. Thus Lafayette Pidge entered the ledgers of town records and though from humble beginnings (he records himself as "toll-keeper" under the occupation required for his marriage certificate), he, like his father, found himself fortunate, for he was to raise seven children on the farm.

The legacy of Lafayette continued to live on in the lore of the tavern. Now named Pidge House and, later, Old Pidge House, the tavern was featured in a number of guides to historic homes in Rhode Island and continued to have visitors throughout the nineteenth century before it was closed in 1901 and sold to the railroad company that ran the trolleys between Providence and Pawtucket.

WASHINGTON AND LITTLE REST

In March 1781, word was sent to Rochambeau in Newport that Commander George Washington desired to travel and meet him in the harbor city. The French counterpart immediately sent his trusted aide, Baron Ludwig Von Closen, to see to every detail of Washington's travel itinerary. Van Closen set out from Newport and rode on horseback through Little Rest and Westerly and then on to Norwich and Lebanon on his way to New Windsor, Connecticut.

The baron was to prove as meticulous to his duty as he was to detail in his journal, and after his much-anticipated meeting with General Washington, he prepared at once to lead the American commander and his aides back to Rhode Island.

On March 2, the party set out from New Windsor, with Washington accompanied by his aides Alexander Hamilton and Tench Tilgham, and started for Newport. After a couple of days of travel, Van Closen rode ahead to inform the townspeople in New Haven and the French troops stationed in Lebanon of the general's impending arrival.

At Little Rest, Van Closen had arranged for eight French cavalry to arrive at Colonel Thomas Potter's inn a full day before Washington's arrival, as the baron was suspicious of the "many Tories in the neighborhood." He let the cavalry know of his concerns for the general's safety and warned that "they would have to guard him carefully during the night."

Washington slept at Potter's tavern on March 5, 1781. The detailed expense accounts of Tilgham show that the general, along with a large party, partook of dinner in the tavern, later retiring to rooms for bed. Others found accommodations at neighboring houses and taverns. All of the party's horses were fed and tended to in Potter's barn.

In a written account left by Colonel Potter's daughter some years after the event, she recalls that the next morning, Washington strolled up and down exploring Main Street without his famous white wig and that he paid for a shave from William Lunt (a soldier and barber in the Rhode Island Militia until the discharge of a defective gun left him wounded), and then he returned to Little Rest.

Washington and his staff, along with a contingent of about twenty soldiers, headed out from Little Rest that morning for the Jamestown ferry. Though his stay was brief, it would have great impact on the community almost immediately. The general's goal in meeting Rochambeau was to free up the French fleet from the harbor so that they could engage the British on the open seas. Rochambeau, as was seen earlier, was reluctant to leave Newport with limited defenses. Washington had informed Colonel Potter at the tavern of the need for additional troops from nearby communities to bolster the French forces.

Within hours of the general's departure, the South Kingston town council was meeting in Potter's Tavern and approved all that Washington had requested. Members voted that local militias have access to guns and cartridges to be stored in a nearby farm and forwarded the request to the General Assembly for an additional five hundred troops to be sent in support of French troops. By May, the State Assembly had ordered that half the men in Rhode Island's independent militias, including those from the Kings County Militia and the Kingston Reds, be stationed outside of Newport. The troops spent the summer camped about four miles out of town and kept the neighboring taverns thriving.

THE GOLDEN BALL TAVERN (MANSION HOUSE) IN PROVIDENCE

Perhaps the most auspicious tavern in Rhode Island associated with this period was one that was opened in the heady days following the war. The Golden Ball Tavern in Providence was established in 1783, across from the Old State House, with much fanfare, advertising spacious rooms and elegant dining. It would soon have occasion to live up to that reputation, for the Marquis de Lafayette had brought from Paris several of his young, aristocratic friends, and they were fêted at some of the finest homes in Providence. But, as Mary Caroline Crawford writes: "Finally, as an event of particular elegance, this party at the Golden Ball was arranged. When the evening arrived, all the beauties of the town were on hand, elegant in rich, flowered brocades over short, quilted petticoats of silk or satin."

The men, she assures us, were "no less gorgeous" in their powdered wigs, satin coats and gold buckled shoes. It seems that that every effort was taken to be sure that it was a night of elegance that would not soon be forgotten, and it was talked of for years after as the "Lafayette Ball."

George Washington would also visit the inn as president during an unexpected visit in 1790. Rhode Island was the last state to ratify the Constitution at this time and was often viewed by outsiders as radically antifederalist, but Washington was determined to visit nonetheless. The

Pennsylvania Packet reported on August 28, 1790, that the president had "arrived in Newport at eight o'clock on Tuesday morning...at which time he was welcomed to the state by a salute from the fort."

The president was greeted by a large crowd of the town's residents and led to the town hall, where an elegant dinner was provided. The newspaper reported that "on Wednesday morning at 9:00 o'clock, the President and his company embarked for Providence." He was welcomed to the city by a large contingent of citizens, including the governor of the state and Senator Foster, along with a large contingent of students from Brown University. William Smith, a member of the president's party, wrote in his diary that "the Governor of the State was so zealous in his respects that he jumped aboard the packet as soon as she got to the wharf to welcome the President." The reception, Williams wrote, was "the same...as at Newport, but the procession to the tavern was more solemn and conducted with a much greater formality, having troops and music."

While there, Washington occupied the same second-story suite that Lafayette had used, and he spent nearly a week in Providence, fêted at a dinner in his honor at the Old State House, where speeches of welcome and cordiality were exchanged despite the political differences at the time. The president humbly told the gathered dignitaries that "America is indebted for freedom and independence, rather to the joint exertions of her citizens of the several States in which it may be your boast to have borne no inconsiderable share, than to the conduct of her Commander-in-Chief."

In 1797, President Adams, on his way to his summer home in Massachusetts, stayed at the Golden Ball. He was welcomed to the city with an enthusiastic gathering of citizens, a salute of cannon fire in his honor and the pealing bells of the First Baptist Church to announce his arrival. While there, he was visited by Esek Hopkins, then eighty-one years old, who had been one of those who commandeered a longboat to the *Gaspee* and then served as the first commander in chief of the American navy. The years and political foes had been unkind to Hopkins after the Revolution, but the reunion between the president who had always praised the commander's gallant conduct and the elderly patriot was said to have brought tears to the old seaman's eyes.

The suite where Washington stayed was opened again for Adams and again later in 1817, when James Madison visited the tavern, now called the Mansion House. Later visitors to the suite included Lafayette during his 1824 tour of New England and the poet James Russell Lowell.

The historic inn underwent several transformations in the years that followed, from the Mansion House to the Roger Williams Hotel, the Ammons

Photo of the Golden Ball Tavern before demolition, circa 1941. *From the author's collection.*

Tavern and the Globe Tavern, among other names, as it fell into "dilapidated dignity behind the old State House" before being demolished in 1941.

These notable establishments and doubtless other taverns throughout the colony played their parts in fomenting the spirit of revolution, providing camaraderie and courage with the cordials imbibed within their walls and later lent the warmth of the hearthside for old veterans to recount those heady days to another generation of Rhode Islanders.

Chapter 5

BULLETS THROUGH THE TAVERN DOOR

The Sprague Tavern and the Dorr Rebellion

In June 1842, the small village of Chepachet, Rhode Island, would become the focal point of a long-simmering dispute that would place its citizens in the heart of what became known as the Dorr Rebellion. Although the portly state senator who was eventually convicted of treason would forever hold the title of instigator, the struggle for reforms he championed began long before he walked the steep hill to the Old State House and took a seat within its chambers.

According to historian J. Stanley Lemons, by the time of the crisis, "Rhode Island had evolved from the most to the least democratic state between 1780 and 1840. Calls for reform began in the 1790s and were repeated in the decades that followed. The malapportionment of seats in the General Assembly was more than matched by the increasing proportions of the disenfranchised."

Rhode Island's charter, granted in 1646, had given landowning freeholders exclusive rights to represent their villages and towns, as well as the right to vote in those communities. As the colony expanded, and especially as urbanization and the flood of immigrants to fill jobs in the new mechanized mills began, the freeholders continued to resist reform. This assembly of "Yankee elites" viewed such reform with a caustic, and often prejudiced, eye, fearful of losing power as well as the prestige that the culture of New

The Old State House, Providence. *Photo by author.*

England had long afforded them. They were increasingly wary of religious upheaval with the influx of Irish Catholics to the mill towns and the growing pools of itinerant laborers who wandered the towns looking for work.

EARLY SUFFRAGISTS

From these early efforts to achieve reform grew Rhode Island's Suffragist Party, a loosely connected body of nonfreeholders, which included poor white laborers, women (who had not yet adopted the name for their own cause), freed slaves and immigrants. It was this body that sought the support of Senator Dorr to press the General Assembly on reforms. This was a tightrope walk for the young representative who came from an affluent family whose mansion can still be seen today on Benefit Street. Despite his family's disapproval, Dorr ardently took up the suffragist cause.

Political rallies and marches were then a novelty in the state, but such actions on the party's part soon sent the first rumblings through the staid assembly. On February 6, 1841, Rhode Island's General Assembly passed an act that called for a convention to "frame a new constitution, in whole or in part, and if only for a constitution in part, that said constitution have under their special consideration the expediency of equalizing the representations of towns in the House of Representatives."

This did little to mollify the Suffragists, for the assembly also declared that such representatives to the convention could, once again, only be freeholders. The party's response to the act reflects its continued skepticism, while acknowledging that "the very fact that such a convention has been ordered proves conclusively that there is a growing disposition on the part of the freeholders of the state to consider and remedy the abuses of its government."

As for the called convention, the party stated that

> *we do not suppose it will do anything for the advancement of freedom in our State. It will be seen that the representation in the convention will be nothing more than a representation of freemen...and therefore we have no more to hope from such a body than we have from the General Assembly. Of course the over-represented towns will send their quota of representatives, and the under-represented towns will be voted down in precisely the same manner as if the General Assembly had themselves taken up the question of a constitution...These contradictions only show the necessity of the people's taking the matter into their own hands...if the General Assembly will not*

The Dorr Estate, Benefit Street, Providence. *Photo by author.*

meet the wants of the People, nor in all probability will a convention acting under them, it is high time [they] took the matter into their own hands, resolved if they cannot obtain redress of their grievances in the ordinary ways, they will take extraordinary measures to obtain it.

Those extraordinary measures were not long in coming. In April 1841, the Suffragist Party held a massive rally, at which an estimated 2,500 to 3,000 people paraded through the streets of Providence, some bearing flags and banners, one of which read "LIBERTY SHALL BE RESTORED TO THE PEOPLE." The following month, in what was generally viewed as concession to the party, the General Assembly passed an act modifying representation. But this act also was "rejected with scorn" by the Suffragists,[41] as a glimpse of the proposed realignment reveals a continued misappropriation: "six delegates from Providence, four from Newport, Warwick, and Smithfield; three each from Tiverton, Bristol, Scituate, North Providence, Coventry, and South Kingston; one each from Jamestown and Barrington; and two each from the other towns; making seventy seven in all."[42]

THE ELECTION OF 1842

As the election year of 1842 approached, the Suffragists set August 28 as the date delegates would be chosen for their convention in small meetings throughout the state. The "People's Convention" then met for its first session on Monday, October 4, and in subsequent meetings on November 12 and again on the 18, members hammered and fashioned a new constitution to be submitted before the people in the general election. In the first paragraph of the proposed constitution, the Suffragists harkened back to Rhode Island's founder and his original intent:

> *In the spirit and in the words of Roger Williams, the illustrious Founder of this State...We declare "that this Government shall be a Democracy" or Government of the People "by the major consent" of the same "only in civil things." The will of the People shall be expressed by Representatives freely chosen, and returning at fixed periods to their constituents. This State shall be, and forever remain, as in the design of its Founder, sacred to "soul liberty," to the rights of conscience, to freedom of thought, of expression, and of action, as hereinafter set forth and secured.*[43]

The Suffragist Party's ambitious plan for reform and a new constitution, which would place all citizens on an equal footing, was not without staunch opposition. The Charter government's "Law and Order" Party undertook a campaign of fear and slander to undermine the suffragists' momentum. As Dr. Patrick Conley writes:

> *One such tactic was the mobilization of the State Militia companies by an Executive Order commanding them to be ready to appear armed and equipped at thirty minutes notice. On 2 April the Assembly passed its "Algerin Law"...this menacing statute imposed severe penalties against those who participated in the upcoming "peoples" election and declared that anyone who assumed state office under the people's constitution was guilty of treason against the State and subject to life imprisonment.*[44]

The campaign had its effect, as some prominent residents of Providence who had supported the proposed "Peoples Constitution" backed away from the Suffragists, and the intimidation of black and Native American voters had untold consequences. By the election in April 1842, the voter turnout was less than it had been at the two conventions. Despite the imposition of Algerin Law, the People's Party held its general election, and Thomas Wilson Dorr prevailed, being elected as the "People's Governor" with 6,359 votes. Two days later, the Charter government held its election, and while the turnout was decidedly less than the voting for the Suffragist platform, the Law and Order Party and its constituents reelected Governor Samuel Ward King. Rhode Island now found itself in the unprecedented position of having, in effect, two separate, elected governing bodies.

AN EMPTY STATEHOUSE ON INAUGURATION DAY

On May 3, 1842, Dorr and a throng of boisterous supporters, fellow elected officials and at least two militia charged with protecting the governor-elect gathered in the square before Hoyles Tavern. They marched in celebratory fashion down Westminister Street, across the bridge over the Moshassuk River to Market Square and on to the old statehouse, only to find the building vacant and the door locked.

Rhode Island, like other states at this time, had several "statehouses" located in various towns to serve as places of assembly for the state's legislature. King and the representatives elected by the freeholders were in Newport, awaiting word of what unfolded in Providence.

As rain fell on the once-enthusiastic crowd outside the locked statehouse door, a decision was made to convene in an unfinished foundry some distance away. Undoubtedly this dampened some enthusiasm, and some in the crowd departed for home, but others followed Dorr and the elected officials to the foundry, where the inaugural session of the People's Government was held that afternoon. They met another day and adjourned, setting another session for July, but by then, the first freely elected Rhode Island government was in danger of falling apart.

Arrests of those who had been elected to the People's Government began almost immediately. Daniel Brown of Newport, Dutee Pearce and Burrington Anthony of Providence were among the first arrested. Welcome B. Sayles, who had been elected Speaker of the House, was also arrested and levied with a heavy fine. Over the next week, others were arrested and charged with treason to the state. Some who were intimidated by the arrests simply walked away from their elected positions and the People's Party. Others, including Dorr, were not so easily intimidated. Pearce and Anthony, after posting bail, slipped away to Washington. Dorr followed a day later, to join them in their appeal to President Tyler.

The visit to Washington was unsatisfactory, Dorr did not mince words about his opinion of Tyler. To the would-be governor, the president was "unequal to his situation and having his mind made up by others." To the fiery reformer, Tyler was simply "casually occupying the place of President."

Dorr also traveled to New York, where he rejected a proposal to let the Charter government stay in power until the courts ruled on the legitimacy of the People's Constitution. While there, Dorr was fêted by the Democratic Party's political machine, a first signal that Rhode Island's predicament was to have national significance. It was in New York, some historians speculate, that Dorr was convinced to return to Providence and take the reins of government by force.

One might have described this as a fiasco, for this is what the "Dorrites," as the papers now called them, met with during their first such attempt. On his return to Providence, Dorr had given a "furious and inflammatory" speech, brandishing a sword given to him in New York. No longer welcomed in his family home, Dorr dutifully accepted the hospitality of Burrington Anthony and made the home his headquarters while he planned the next maneuver.

THE DORRITES' ERRANT PLAN

While in New York, an arrest warrant had been issued for Dorr, though amnesty was offered by King to those other elected officials if they would swear allegiance to the Charter government. When Dorr learned that a number of legislators and supporters took advantage of the offer, it surely caused him no little consternation and perhaps made him eager to reassert his right to govern.

After much debate, a plan was formed to attack and occupy the state arsenal, then located at Dexter Field in the west end of town. A detachment of men was sent to College Hill, where the United Train Artillery Company was located. Many in the militia were loyal to Dorr, the unit being made up of mechanics and Irish laborers who had voted for the People's Government. A pair of cannons were requisitioned and taken across town, where they were positioned in front of Anthony's house, along with other pieces of artillery. As if to justify their plan of action, the Dorrites issued a broadside on May 16, proclaiming that "A Horrible Plot to drench the State of Rhode Island with the Blood of its Inhabitants" had been uncovered in King's letter to Tyler, asking for Federal troops to shoot down "the peaceable inhabitants...for having dared to exercise the dearest rights of free citizens."

Nineteenth-century photograph of the Burrington Anthony House. *From Mowry's* The Dorr War.

By May 17, Governor Samuel Ward King issued his own broadside, appealing to the citizens of Providence to "Repair to the State Arsenal and Take Arms." By nightfall, the arsenal was filled with militia loyal to the Law and Order Party, as well as armed volunteers, including Dorr's father, brother and brother-in-law. At about 1:00 a.m., at a signal fired from one of the guns on Anthony's lawn, a procession of some three hundred men, led by Dorr, marched to the arsenal. The night was shrouded in a dense fog, and Dorr gave command to Colonel Wheeler, who had the men fan out on both sides of the building while the cannons were positioned to face the front. A Colonel Carter was sent to the door, brandishing a white kerchief wrapped around his sword as a sign of truce, to demand surrender of the arsenal. He was answered by a defiant reply, and soon the small army outside began to hear the preparation of the guns inside the arsenal to be fired upon them. One commander from Pawtucket withdrew his troops immediately, and others around Colonel Wheeler soon felt their courage abate when they realized the arsenal would not be surrendered without a fight.

Dorr ordered one of the cannons to be fired. It smoked and sputtered, but nothing more. The second cannon also failed to fire. Perhaps the powder had been dampened by the mist and fog, perhaps the cannons were simply too old for use, having been captured from the British during the Revolutionary War. Whatever the reason, Dorr quickly realized that they were of no use in this revolution and retreated before the sun rose above Dexter Field.

Regrouping in Chepachet

With this setback, the Dorrites, as the *Journal* now called the suffragists, scattered and regrouped quietly in secluded locations as a price was soon levied on their heads for acts of treason. Dorr met with advisors in Woonsocket, where Jedediah Sprague "appointed a committee to select a ground suitable for military exercise." Dorr went on to New York and Connecticut to confer with sympathizers there, while Sprague and others worked to assemble forces in the small, farming village of Chepachet.

It likely came as no surprise that this village would be chosen for the rendezvous of troops and citizens loyal to the People's Constitution. A significant number of its citizens, especially those proprietors of the meetinghouse, held a long history of supporting the suffragist cause.

Records of the meetinghouse indicate that fifteen of sixty-five members, roughly one-third of the proprietors, had voted for the new constitution, including Nelson Eddy, Asa Hawkins and Jedediah Sprague.

Sprague was a prominent person in town; not only did he hold a place in the meetinghouse, but he was also the owner of the Chepachet Hotel, known informally as the Sprague Tavern. Bought from Cyrus Cooke four years before the events of 1842, the house, as other taverns, had long been the site of town meetings and civil affairs.

After the early June meeting in Woonsocket, the Sprague Tavern became the headquarters of the Dorr advisors. Though in his deposition two years after the events, Sprague downplayed his own role and the role of the tavern in the rebellion, documents from Dorr are addressed to "General Sprague," and he and the other military advisors chose Acote's Hill, just south of the village for the gathering of a military force.

On Wednesday, June 22, a small militia from Woonsocket arrived, hauling a cannon into the peaceful village, causing immediate excitement and a

Nineteenth-century photograph of the Sprague Tavern. *Courtesy of the Chepachet Free Will Baptist Church.*

gathering of the curious. More cannons and troops arrived during the day, and by the following morning, militia loyal to Dorr, volunteers from the Suffragist Party and other seekers of adventure began to encamp on the hillside. Dorr arrived in town early Saturday morning and took rooms in the Sprague Tavern. Upon visiting the encampment later that day, he must have been struck by how inaccurate the estimates of the men gathered that had been sent to him in Connecticut had been. The newspapers touting the rebellion had also overestimated the gathering force, with the *Journal* printing that six hundred men had encamped outside the village and the *Express* reporting that seven hundred troops awaited the Charter government's forces.

Dorr found less than two hundred soldiers on the hill or guarding the village. The remainder of those encamped seemed to be "spectators, stragglers and hangers on." Despite this, Dorr gave a rousing speech to those gathered on the hill, declaring that he would "rather leave his bones whitening on Acote's Hill than deny the people their rights." He issued a summons to the legislature elected to the People's Government to convene in Sprague's Tavern "for the transaction of such business as may come before them."

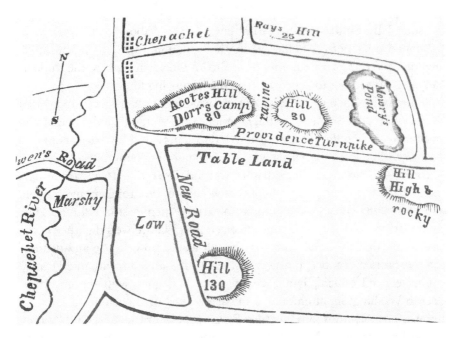

Map of Chepachet showing Acote's Hill encampment. *Courtesy of the Rhode Island Historical Society.*

These optimistic actions aside, Dorr must have been troubled by the small force gathered with little experience, as well as the circumstances in which he found himself and his followers.

Early on that first morning of encampment, a patrol of volunteers had captured four armed men on the road leading to the village. These men were taken to be an advanced guard for the larger force expected to arrive, as intelligence that had come on the stagecoaches the day before had told of armed militia gathering in the city for an attack on Chepachet. After the men were captured, the forces on Acote's Hill fired cannons to deter any other reconnaissance from approaching and hastily marched the prisoners to Woonsocket, where they were discharged, while the volunteers, with a few added men, returned to the village.

In Providence, militia and volunteers loyal to the Charter government were indeed gathering. According to Mowry's account, on "Saturday morning, three hundred and fifty men arrived in Providence—the artillery companies from Newport, Bristol and Warren and the steamboat at once returned to Newport for the remainder of the militia of that town; a body of four hundred men arrived on the railroad, from the southern part of the state." By Sunday, with martial law declared, about 1,300 men were encamped on Jefferson Plains, while the remaining army of about 3,000 men quartered in private homes or at Brown University, where the students had been turned out to accommodate the occupying forces.

Saturday in Chepachet was spent improving the scant fortifications that had been erected on Acote's Hill. Cannon were brought up the height and positioned to face the road from Providence. Dorr and his advisors met in the tavern under an increasingly ominous cloud of doubt and uncertainty. According to Sprague, the advisors warned Dorr that they increasingly "believed that the village of Chepachet would not be strong enough to hold out against any considerable number of armed men or strong force." Dorr continued to hold out hope that the elected legislature would gather in the tavern and that the small force on the hill would prove to be an adequate defense. From a distance, however, others saw the situation with more clarity.

One elected official, Dutee Pearce, who had gone with the governor-elect to Washington, attempted to persuade Dorr of the fruitlessness of his actions. The Algerans, or Governor King's supporters, he told him, had put forward a measure, where all could vote for representation, and many of those suffragist supporters "were quite willing to accept this proposition as a compromise of the difficulties."

Dorr initially refused to back down, even when told by Pearce that he could expect a heavily armed force from Providence within a few days. On Monday, Dorr's father and younger brother visited and once again attempted to dissuade "the poor deluded son" from his ambitions. Their remains no record of the meeting, but by Monday afternoon, word had been given to dismantle the forces on Acote's Hill. Dorr sent a message by coach to Walter S. Burges in Providence, requesting that he publish the notice of disbandment in the *Express*, long regarded as the mouthpiece of the Suffragist Party. And so it seemed the "Battle for Acote's Hill," as the papers came to call it, was over before it had even begun.

As we shall see, however, the incident was to leave a lasting mark on the history of the town, and the shame of infamy on the state government was yet to come.

THE TAVERN AND TOWN VIOLATED

Dorr and his advisors left Chepachet in the early evening. The following morning, at about 7:45 a.m., the remaining stragglers on Acote's Hill were duly rounded up and the abandoned cannons confiscated by the Charter troops under command of Colonel William Brown. And while "a fair number of shots were fired at the site of encampment," they were mainly to scatter the crowd of mostly young boys of the town who had gathered to watch the arrival of troops from Providence.

After the hill was secured, the militias began to occupy the town, commandeering the Pettingill-Mason House at the foot of the hill to serve as a field hospital, then moving on to the houses, barns and the storefronts in town, confiscating any weapons found and arresting those suspected of conspiring with Dorr. At about seven o'clock, a contingent of troops arrived at the tavern. Jedediah Sprague, who left a lengthy deposition, recalled the scene at his inn that morning:

> *There were in my house at the time said advance guard arrived, only eight male persons, besides my own family and domestics, three of these were gentlemen from Boston who had arrived that morning; one gentleman from Long Island, and three persons with him, who had stopped overnight as travelers, and who had not, to my knowledge, had anything to do with the matters at that time agitating the State; and a Mr. Lyman Cooley, who had left the village the night before, and had returned that morning to my house, through fear, as he stated that he could not make his escape.*

As the carriages of the troops pulled up before the tavern, a considerable crowd gathered and continued to grow, though no one was apparently armed. Sprague told the court that "none of the persons in my house were, to my knowledge, in any way armed; there was no such instrument as a musket, gun, pistol, sword, or the like, to be seen in said house."

Growing increasingly alarmed, Sprague climbed out a side window of the tavern and made his way to the front door, where an awkward confrontation seems to have taken place. He invited the commander of the guard to enter the house, but instead, a soldier blocked the door with his musket, as though to prevent anyone from either entering or leaving the premises. As the crowd mustered about the entrance, Nelson Eddy, who had wanted to enter the house, brazenly raised the musket and stepped inside. The enraged guard then lowered his musket again and aimed it at the door, demanding that Eddy come out or he would "shoot him down." Sprague attempted to fend off the guard, but as he describes:

> *There was a general rush at this time of the armed soldiers and unarmed citizens and spectators for the doorway, and the entry was immediately filled*

with both classes—the armed soldiers attempting to shoot the unarmed and continually keeping up the cry of "Godamn em' shoot em' down." I was in the midst of this scene, and was continually raising and brushing off the muskets, pistols. Carbines, &c., with which they were armed; commanding them not to shoot; telling them that they were not resisted by any armed force.

Tensions began to escalate. Sprague went back inside to find a number of unarmed persons blocking the door from being broken in. One of the soldiers broke a window and thrust a pistol inside, but he did not fire. Sprague made his way out another window and climbed out to confront John T. Pitman, whose musket was still trained on the tavern door.

"For God's sake, don't fire in there," Sprague testified to yelling, but Pitman reportedly retorted, "I don't care a Goddamn, I mean to kill somebody," and fired into the house. The unlucky recipient of Pitman's musket ball was George H.N. Bardine, who suffered "a deep and severe flesh wound" in the thigh.

Once Pitman had fired, the tavern was occupied quickly and in a ruthless manner. "The soldiers who took possession of my house," Sprague told the court, "were abusive and rough in their language and their behavior, from the time they entered, as aforesaid…they took possession of every room in the house, and of all my effects, and ransacked from garret to cellar."

The charter troops ensconced themselves in Sprague's tavern, also taking possession of his barn and stable with its six horses. They opened the tavern bar and "helped themselves to cigars, wines and ardent spirits according to their pleasure; several hundred dollars worth of property was consumed or destroyed."

Other houses in the village and other citizens met with the same intrusion and ransacking of their property. Asa Hawkins described how, earlier that morning, he and his sons were "engaged in hoeing opposite my house…when a detachment of Charter troops appeared on said road."

The troops halted "about thirty rods" from the house and sent a few armed men into the field to question Hawkins. They inquired about the small charcoal cabins on his neighbor's property, took him to his house and questioned him about the strength of Dorr's force. They searched the house and then led him to his barn across the road. Hawkins willingly let a soldier inside and watched as he "proceeded to make a close search for something buried in the hay, thrusting his bayonet into the mow in various places. He however, succeeded in stabbing nothing but one beam, which he did very spitefully—thinking, as I supposed, that he had found a Dorrite."

The procession of prisoners to Providence. *From an engraving by H. Lord, printed in Burke's report.*

Over the coming days, similar searches were conducted throughout the village. The Charter troops continued the "sacking" of Chepachet in similar fashion. At Ripsy Tift's home, the soldiers made off with several household items, including silver, a cookstove and even a pair of "lasting garters." The searches and manhandling went on outside the village as well. Houses were searched in Cumberland as suspected Dorrite hideouts, even as far as Bellingham, Massachusetts, where a tavern in town was searched for escaping conspirators. Under the guise of martial law, the Charter troops menaced and terrified ordinary citizens. By Mowry's account, generally regarded to be sympathetic to the Charter, "During the forty days that martial law was in full operation,…Hundreds of men were held in 'durance vile'; hundreds of houses were searched for hidden weapons, or men." By Wednesday afternoon in Chepachet, troops had arrested more than one hundred persons and roped them together in groups of eight—"the rope…passed in a clove hitch around each man's arm, passing behind his back, and fastening him close up to his neighbor"—and in this way prepared them for the long march to Providence.

According to witnesses, the men were continually prodded with bayonets to keep them moving the twelve miles along the turnpike to the city.

Once they reached the city, the prisoners were halted before Hoyles Tavern, where so many had optimistically gathered for Dorr's inauguration months before. They were led through the streets, past jeering crowds of Algerine supporters, and spit upon, with some of the troops taunting the prisoners that they were being led to College Hill to be shot.

DORR'S LEGACY

In the end, the conduct of the Charter troops and their treatment of the state's citizens was to sully the governor and the Charter government's reputation far greater than any words or actions that had yet taken place during the conflict for a new constitution. In hearings that began in July, the full account of the indiscriminate methods of arrest, the depravations deposed on suspected Dorrites and the treatment of the prisoners by the military began to be published. While the Charter government continued to utilize the newspapers to propagandize the trials of "the traitors" and the fact that Dorr himself was still at large, the ultimate tribunal of public opinion had swayed to those citizens who had willingly placed themselves in danger for the cause of liberty.

During the November following the events in Chepachet and the counties around the village, the citizens of Rhode Island overwhelmingly approved a new constitution, which included a bill of rights, established an independent judiciary, reined in the power of the legislature and gave blacks the right to vote. In short, Dorr and his supporters may have lost the Battle for Acote's Hill, but they were victorious in their war to keep alive the American ideal of democracy.

A curious footnote to this episode in Rhode Island history is a finding in a 1929 guide to historical places in the state that mentions that those who fled Chepachet in the aftermath of the "invasion" went to Cumberland and stayed in a large cavern for several weeks at a place called "Rocky Dundee," just north of the reservoir. I have hiked many times on the trail adjacent to this area and have seen, with binoculars, the likely place this cave would be, but the area is now protected and well guarded, as it is the primary water source for much of Pawtucket.

Chapter 6

SPIRITS OF ANOTHER KIND

The state of Rhode Island, being one of the earliest settlements with some of the oldest houses in New England, would naturally become known for having more than its share of restless spirits wandering within, and sometimes without, those old dwellings.

Taverns and inns, especially, became places of storied memory, full of tales that would transform into legends over time, and these tales often grew when the old houses were abandoned. One such house was the old Battey Tavern in Warwick. In a story relayed by Horace Belcher, the tavern had been known to be haunted for some time when he was a young boy in the town. One day, a man leading a wagon past the old place stopped and explored the house for the cause of the mysterious noises he heard. He found a door creaking back and forth with the breeze that came through a windowless frame, and he laughed at himself and the old stories he'd heard in town. But that did not sway the children who trotted quickly past the tavern on their way home from school on those darkening autumn days.

In a number of these inns and taverns that still offer hospitality, the perpetual guests who roam the halls and visit rooms are a part of the history of those houses, and some are still making themselves known to be here with us in the present day.

The White Horse Tavern, Newport. *Photo by author.*

GHOSTS HARBORED IN NEWPORT

The oldest existing tavern in the state of Rhode Island is also the site of one of the oldest known hauntings in New England. For generations in the White Horse Tavern, kitchen workers, hired maids and helpers and the proprietors themselves have all encountered an old man in shabby colonial clothes who most often appears on the right-hand side of the dining room fireplace or in the rooms upstairs.

Former curator Anita Rafael told the *Rhode Island Monthly* magazine of an encounter in recent years. A family with a young boy had come in and was having lunch in the tavern one late afternoon. Eventually, the boy became fidgety and asked to use the bathroom. He was directed to the guest bathroom in the upstairs corner of the house. The boy didn't come down for a long time, though the parents could hear footsteps circling around upstairs, and they assumed that he was just exploring. But this went on, and when he finally did come down, the parents, as you might expect, questioned the boy as to his adventure.

He told them, as they'd guessed, that he'd been circling around the massive chimney through the rooms upstairs, but he also told him that he was in the presence of an old man who sometimes followed him and sometimes just watched him in this game. The parents became worried and attracted the attention of the nearby staff. They questioned the boy again in their presence. As Ms. Rafael describes the scene:

> *They were worried and started really questioning the boy. Well, what did he look like, and what was he wearing, and where did he go? And the little kid said, "Well, he was an old guy, and he had an old coat, an old fashioned coat, and old fashioned clothes and things like that."*
>
> *At this point the waiters were bug-eyed, because they knew what the little kid had seen, and that it was the figure that they themselves had seen in the past: a guy, an older man, in old-fashioned clothes, old coat, old boots, old hat.*

In her time working as curator, Ms. Rafael found a possible explanation for the haunting by tracing this apparition to an unfortunate guest who had spent his first night in the tavern in the 1720s. The house was owned at the time by Robert and Mary Nichols, who provided food and shared lodging for travelers to the city by the sea. One late evening, two travelers arrived together and took a shared room. When the men did not come down to breakfast the following morning, Mrs. Nichols sent a local Narragansett girl who worked for her upstairs to wake them. The girl found that one of the men had simply vanished, and the other lay dead on the floor by the fireplace.

In the brief investigation that followed, authorities found no signs of a struggle or wounds of any kind on the man's body. Fearing that his sudden death and the mysterious disappearance of the other stranger might be signs of some dreaded disease, they buried the man quickly in a pauper's grave and sent Mary Nichols and the Narragansett girl into quarantine. Unhappily, both of them came down with smallpox from being housed with infected people on Coaster's Harbor Island, where the War College resides now. A newspaper article from the time reported that "the wife of the innkeeper, Robert Nichols, at the Nichol's Tavern…has lately returned to her duties as the innkeeper's wife after a bout of smallpox."

The article relayed the story of her encounter with the two strangers, the unexplained death and the mysterious disappearance of the other traveler. It sent a plea to readers who might know the man, his whereabouts and

An old postcard of the Hotel Viking. *Courtesy of the Providence Public Library.*

what occurred to contact the authorities, but this unexplained death and the identity of the men have apparently never been resolved. Despite this detail about the case and the recovery of Mary Nichols, the paper fails to mention the related death of the innocent Indian girl who took those fateful steps upstairs and first opened the door to this mystery.

Another colonial entity appears frequently in an old Newport house that was recently converted into a restaurant called Le Petit Auberge, where a cook reported seeing a man in a colonial uniform seated in one of the rooms upstairs, and other staff have seen the apparition in other locations of the house. The ghost is said to be that of the Revolutionary War naval commander Stephen Decatur, whose childhood home the restaurant now occupies. Decatur died young in a duel, and it may be that his last thoughts were of his Newport home. Aside from making an occasional appearance, the commander does little more to disturb patrons than rattling the silverware on the dining tables from time to time.

Newport has other spirits haunting the town's old inns and taverns. When a portion of the luxurious Agassiz Mansion was turned into an upscale bed-and-breakfast, the owners found that a restless female apparition wanders the halls and rooms in a seemingly agitated state. In the pantry, dishes will sometimes fly from the shelves without warning.

The Pilgrim House Inn, Newport. *Photo by author.*

The opulent Hotel Viking is host to an ongoing party whose celebratory noise often disturbs guests, an apparent cacophony of music and laughter that long emanated from an unused part of the old building. Since renovations occurred several years ago, the old room used for storage is in use again, and the din seems to have calmed in the old hotel.

The three-storied Pilgrim Inn, with its large deck overlooking the town and harbor, reportedly has the spirit of a mischievous little girl in the midst of its staff and patrons. The buzzing of the intercom from empty rooms, slamming of the dryer door and other practical jokes have been reported by the housekeepers. In rooms 8 and 11, the shadow of an image has appeared, as has the sound of laughter, and in one instance, a music box was heard coming from a locked and empty chamber. One guest who had stayed in room 8 wrote in the journal provided by the inn: "I don't know if you'll believe me, but this room is haunted." But of course the owners and staff already knew. One intuitive housekeeper had named the spirit "Jessica" long ago, and that's what they have called her ever since.

One summer night, a tour group passing by the inn noticed a little girl in old-fashioned clothes standing in the doorway. They excitedly inquired at the inn whether there were any children staying at the present time, and finding that there were not, they left convinced that the vision they had witnessed vanish from the stairway was the little girl of legend. No one knows for sure who "Jessica" is, though there is speculation that she may be the youngest daughter of the Curren family, who lived in the house in the nineteenth century. Perhaps, as the guest mused upon leaving, the spirit of the little girl is simply "looking for someone she knows."

SPECTERS IN THE CAPITAL CITY

Providence, the state's other colonial city, also has a number of apparitions walking the old streets above the river and dwelling in the elegant homes of the East Side and a few college halls of Brown University as well. Most of the city's oldest taverns and inns have been lost to fire or torn down in the last century. Such were the fates of the old Mowry Tavern, demolished in 1900, the famous Golden Ball in 1941 and the Old Pidge House in 1954.

The city's oldest existing hotel, however, is home to more than a few tales of haunting and unusual occurrences, but then, as some claim, the building has been under a dark cloud since its inception. The Biltmore Hotel was opened in 1922 by Johan Leisse Weisskopf, a wealthy, self-indulgent

The famous Bacchante Dining Room of the Providence Biltmore. *Courtesy of the Providence Public Library.*

businessman who was also reputed to be a follower of Aleister Cowley, the well-known Satanist. Weisskopf was also reputed to be on friendly terms with the local mafia, and this, perhaps more than anything else, contributed to the Biltmore's early success.

Decadence was in the design of the hotel itself, from the hot springs in the basement to the soon-to-be-famous Bacchante Dining Room, whose exclusive guests were served drinks by their waitresses who were fully undressed, save for their serving aprons. Scott and Zelda Fitgerald, Douglas Fairbanks and Louis Armstrong were among the luminaries drawn to the Biltmore's dazzling décor and lavish parties.

During Prohibition, Rhode Island was among those states that took a decidedly lenient stand on enforcing the nations anti-drinking laws. Wine was liberally served to Biltmore patrons, along with other spirits. Police and city officials often stopped at the bar for a free drink, a policy that ensured the owner's protection, but this period also proved to be one of the most violent and corrupt in the hotel's history. It's likely that these are the spirits that reportedly still haunt the hotel today, which was extensively renovated in the 1990s while the city created its now-famous Riverwalk and basin, and the Biltmore remains an iconic fixture in the city's landscape and a popular tourist destination.

Among the hauntings reported, the sound of raucous parties has been heard by guests for decades, as well as locked doors suddenly unlocking, the sound of laughter and moving orbs, especially on the sixteenth floor, as well as the apparition of a female spirit. In his book *Haunted Providence*, mentalist Rory Raven also reports sightings of an unfortunate stockbroker who plunged to his death from the fourteenth floor on Black Tuesday in 1929. The room where he stayed is reputedly haunted, and guests are sometimes startled by the unsettling vision of a man falling past their windows to the street below.

The Ruffstone Tavern in North Providence is an establishment with a long history, having served as a pub, a stop on the Underground Railroad and a speakeasy during

Postcard of the Providence Biltmore. *From the author's collection.*

Prohibition. Its origins date back to about 1778, and the present and previous owners have long been subjected to a variety of spirit activity. The tavern is host to a female apparition who makes staff and patrons aware of her presence by the musky scent of her perfume that will suddenly permeate a room. Heavy doors will suddenly swing open or closed, dishes and bottles will mysteriously fall from their places and the apparition of a man in a top hat, holding a pipe, has also been reported. Such was the frequency of activity that the owners called in the famous ghost hunters from The Atlantic Paranormal Society (TAPS) to investigate, though in the three days that they spent at the tavern, they found little of consequence. A most interesting side note to the spirit activity is the report that the basement of the tavern once held a tunnel (long since boarded up) that led into the city of Providence.

THE HAUNTED INN OF CHEPACHET

Rural villages and towns in Rhode Island often hold an even longer history of spirits and sightings. We have only to return to Chepachet and the site of the Sprague Tavern mentioned in the previous chapter to determine this. Over time, the tavern changed owners and names from the Chepachet Inn to the Glocester Hotel and the Stage Coach Inn, to its present name of Tavern on the Main.

This house, so steeped in Rhode Island history, is the home of numerous spirits and is, undoubtedly, one of the most haunted places in the state. For many years, there have been tales of a little boy disappearing in the ladies room, as well as the apparition of a female spirit in old-fashioned dress who is said to appear in the last booth in the back of the dining room, an entity tied to an infamous murder by a jealous man on Valentine's Day.

In recent times, the old tavern has been the scene of several paranormal investigations, and the evidence has revealed even more spirits than were previously known to exist and confirmed the local lore of a place haunted by its long and violent past.

Some years ago, a curious discovery also fueled speculation about the tavern. In 1998, during renovations to the centuries-old foundation, workers uncovered a beautifully preserved nineteenth-century sawed-off shotgun that had been wrapped in oilcloth and buried about a foot deep beside the wall. The inscribed initials F.J.W. showed that the gun belonged to Frederick J. Williams, who had been employed by the Providence-Worchester Stage Coach line in the early 1800s. The tavern, then the Glocester Hotel, would have been a frequent stop, but why he buried his gun on the premises is a mystery that remains unsolved.

Among evidence gathered in these recent investigations, the apparition of a "female" shadow was captured on camera, floating through the dining room, and ghostly orbs were filmed in the bathroom where the little boy has been seen. Perhaps it is this little boy's voice that was captured by the East Coast Paranormal Research Team when an investigator called out the name of a suspected spirit and asked the empty room, "Is that you?" A child's voice answers, in a distinctly anguished cry, "No, no, we're all dead!"

Those spirits inhabiting the tavern along with the boy and female spirit include several male entities that testify to events during the tavern's more raucous nights, when it served as a stagecoach destination. One captured electronic voice phenomenon (EVP) is of a male who states matter-of-factly, "The third bullet killed him. Check the couch." Another voice seems to be

Signboard of the Stage Coach Tavern, Chepachet. *Photo by the author.*

that of a man from the colonial era, seemingly annoyed with the investigators' presence, as he tersely tells him, "I will cut you. Goodbye." And perhaps most sinister is the spirit seemingly intent on murder whose threats can be heard amid the cacophony of other voices.

Despite the evidence gathered here of a less-than-calm spirit atmosphere, there is little, if any, evidence that any actual harm has been done to patrons. A television set famously fell to the floor when one patron remained skeptical about the stories told, and one investigative team witnessed a crystal glass explode on a table while they were there. The tavern operates as a restaurant, whose décor seems little changed from a nineteenth-century setting, and the bar, whose patrons are now mostly tourists and curious day travelers, is still a lively taproom, as it was in the stagecoach and carriage days. Only one thing seems to have changed in the running of the house from Cyrus Cooke's time, and that is that, with good reason, the upstairs rooms are no longer rented for the night.

THE LEGEND OF THE "INDIAN ROOM"

Another old tavern is home to one of the earliest legends in the state. The Black Horse Tavern, as it was known in the 1700s, at the time this legend began, was already a well-known tavern in Scituate. By the time that Reuben Jenckes inherited the house from his uncle, it had been a tavern since his grandfather's days. The house rested on the old Danielson Pike, a popular stagecoach and carriage route from neighboring Connecticut. It had several small rooms for rent and a long taproom just a few steps from the intersection of the Pike and Coventry Road. A large carriage house in back gave respite to the weary horses while the drivers and passengers imbibed at the bar.

It was but a short distance from the Pine Tree Tavern, but as there were many other such establishments the length of the turnpike, the owners of the Black Horse felt that traffic on the road was enough to keep both places in the village well occupied. But shortly after Jenckes moved his family into the house, a series of disturbances began.

Travelers sleeping in a certain room complained of a terrifying visit from a Native American spirit who, in each story, "buried his hand in the sleeper's hair" and then lifted his or her head from the pillow while holding a raised tomahawk above the terrified captive. This became such a common occurrence that the chamber became known as the "Indian Room," and according to a turn-of-the-century guide to the state, "although this chamber was rented at a lesser rate than other rooms, few who knew the story connected to it would sleep there."[45]

People in the village told Jenckes that the ghost was an old "hanger-on" at the Pine Tree Tavern, and in loyalty, they supposed, he was determined to drive customers from the rival inn by whatever means his spirit could muster. But the spirit also plagued Jenckes's wife and daughter with dreams. In an early dream reported by Jenckes's wife, the ghost "pulled off her nightcap, seized her by the hair, pulled her down the stairs and through the front door and pointed angrily to the roots of a large cedar tree that grew by the front gate, muttering in broken English of his need to avenge some insult to his race."

When the terrified mistress of the house informed her husband of the dream, he interpreted the Indian's gestures as revealing the place of a long-hidden treasure and immediately dug around the entire base of the old tree, but he found nothing. When the spirit next visited Mrs. Jenckes and took her outside, he pointed to the base of the cedar on the other side of the gate. Again, the owner dug but found nothing there. On another visit, the native spirit led Mrs. Jenckes to the apple orchard and pointed out a particularly

The Black Horse Tavern, as seen today. *Photo by author.*

prized tree. Rueben dug once more but again found nothing. Despite these fruitless efforts, Jenckes continued to dig for treasure after each reported dream, until he had destroyed nearly half of his orchard.

Legend has it that Jenckes finally gave up his search for treasure, but the spirit kept returning to Mrs. Jenckes over the years, repeating his story that he had suffered an insult so grave that it would not let him have peace. Mrs. Jenckes, it seems, was determined to decipher the meaning of these visits.

One night, the Indian came to the daughter in a dream and led her to a low-lying shed on the property that was packed with decades of discarded and forgotten items: empty barrels, pieces of furniture, assorted storage bins and a trunk, which the spirit pointed out in a far corner of the loft. To eleven-year-old Lucy, it looked eerily like a coffin. When she told her mother the dream and pointed out the trunk in the loft to her, Mrs. Jenckes shooed her daughter away and enlisted a pair of the female help from the tavern to unpack the loft. What they found was an old trunk bound with fraying rope, and inside, a body, or half of one. In fact, it was the hardwood torso and head of a mannequin, with a set of pins and the other implements of a wig-making kit.

Reuben recognized it at once when it was brought to him. It seems his grandfather was a wigmaker in the days when he owned the house, as a sideline to his duties as tavern keeper. The wearing of wigs in this day would have been a daily fashion for many, the same as pulling on a shirt in the morning, and a traveler, especially, would likely be inclined to add a new hairpiece to his collection.

Versions of the story vary as to what was done with the find, but needless to say, it was properly disposed of, having surmised that the native must have suffered his humiliation in the act of attempting to scalp one of these travelers, perhaps in the tavern itself, and was left holding, instead, a bloodless wig in his hand.

Shortly after this incident, the family joined with friends in a migration to Ohio, and the tavern was sold. Apparently, the native spirit never showed himself again, and the tavern continued for many years, though by the early twentieth century, it had declined, some would say, to a house of disreputable character. Even the present-day owners can tell you stories from those spirited, if not ghostly, nights.

SOUTH COUNTY SPIRITS

An old house in South County with a long reputation for haunting is the General Stanton Inn of Charlestown. Built on the tract of land given to General Thomas Stanton in 1655, the house is one of the oldest in town,

The General Stanton Inn, as seen today. *Photo by author.*

and in its early stages, it served as a schoolhouse to Stanton's children and the neighboring Native Americans. Rooms were eventually added to the original structure, with the last addition being made in 1740 by the general's nephew, Joseph Stanton. After the Revolutionary War, the house was opened as a tavern, with a dining room named the "Washington Cabinet Room" and a larger "Williamsburg" room. The house soon became a popular stop on the stagecoach run between New London and Providence.

While most activity in the old house has been merely mischievous, the appearance of a male apparition, dressed in a white shirt with brown pants and an old farmer's hat, has occurred numerous times. A little girl, believed to be Stanton's youngest daughter, who died in the house, also appears in the rooms and sometimes leaves her fingerprints on the old windowpanes. The most recent owner of the inn, Janice Falcon, has told me that a guest once sent her a photograph of herself taken peering around a doorframe in the house. On the other side of the frame in the photo, one can clearly see the shoulder of a uniform adorned with epaulets.

These occurrences and the sensations of being touched, felt by both staff and patrons in the rooms, have been so prevalent that paranormal experts were called in to investigate. As with the tavern in Chepachet, investigations revealed more spirits in the house, including EVPs of an old woman humming, and the voice of a child, perhaps that of the little girl previously seen, was recorded in the attic.

HAUNTS ON NEW SHOREHAM

The village of New Shoreham, better known as Block Island to mainlanders, is as spirited a place as any in Rhode Island. For a time, Roger Williams and William Coddington rented the island from the Narragansett for the keeping of sheep. A century later, the island was home to a rough-hewn and stubborn few inhabitants, who farmed the inland fields, salvaged the wrecks that gathered off Sandy Point and fished the Atlantic well past the season for reasonable men to put themselves at risk of a sudden gale in Long Island Sound.

As the decades progressed, the island's remoteness and pristine beaches attracted entrepreneurs who built the grand hotels that New Yorkers and the elite from Boston and Connecticut demanded when they vacationed from the city. Most of the ghostly sightings in the island's old inns and hotels seem to be spirits from this era, but again, these are the sightings in places that still exist today, and beyond the beachfront hotels, other houses are reputed to be haunted as well.

Of these grand hotels, the New Shoreham House would seem to have more than its share of otherworldly guests. The sounds of furniture being dragged across the floor, a sudden smell of sulfur in one room whose bed also occasionally shakes violently and locks being inverted so that the room is impossible to enter, are all fairly common occurrences in the old hotel. But most persistent has been the apparition of a little girl to numerous people over the years.

In her book *Block Island Ghosts*, local author and year-round resident Fran Migliaccio recounts the experiences of recent owners Bob and Kathy Schleimer. Initially, the vision of the little girl came to their two-year-old daughter, then sleeping in room 2 of the hotel. This happened most often at night, but occasionally, during the day, Bob would hear his daughter having a conversation with someone and, upon finding her alone, discover that she had been talking with her "friend," who, she said, had been there only a moment ago.

As he soon found, the little girl also appeared to guests. One visitor from Philadelphia was especially distraught and left after spending only one night. A couple of years later, she called the owners and told them that the one night she had spent in their hotel had changed her life. She had never believed in ghosts, she told them, but that night, the apparition of a little girl had appeared and told her that she was looking for her mother. The experience had profoundly affected the woman and caused her to reevaluate her beliefs. She felt she was a more religious person because of it. Later that year, the woman returned to the New Shoreham House and stayed for three days in room 2, communicating with the little girl at will, entirely at peace.

Perhaps the most remarkable experience was that of a chambermaid named Patty, who worked at the hotel in the summer of 1987. The owners recalled that

> Patty had been sleeping upstairs one night, and in the morning she came to us and told us that during the night, a mist had come into her room, under the door, and had formed into the image of a little girl. The little girl held out her hand and told Patty to hold on to it. Patty did, and found herself drifting over Block Island with this little girl, who kept telling her, "you're safe, you're safe." And she was conducted safely back to her room.[46]

The following year, a man named Barrie Konicov appeared on the hotel's doorstep and told the Schleimers that he had been "given a message" to help spirits in the house pass along to the next world. He was led to room 2, where he stayed for some hours, communicating with the spirits. When he came out, he told the owners that he had helped an old sea captain who resided in the hotel and frequently roamed Mohegan Bluffs looking for his lost dog. He also had an encounter with the little girl, but he was unable to locate the spirit of the mother she has been searching for all these years.

In the three-storied Highview Inn, the rooms were given ships' names, and on the third floor, in and around a room named the Atalanta, strange and inexplicable events occur on a regular basis. Drafts go through the room while the windows are shut, and chimes ring out when there is no breeze to stir them. Sudden changes in temperature and odd noises are common. One day, a young woman had left the door to the room open and saw the apparition of a young girl who seemed to float right past the opened door. Another visitor several years later was lying on the bed reading a newspaper when the paper was suddenly ripped in half.

Old postcard of Block Island Hotels. *From the author's collection.*

A speech pathologist who stayed in the Highview each time she came to visit the school on the island told the owners that she often felt a female presence next her on the stairs to her room, but whenever she attempted a greeting, it would disappear.

Another tenant for a time told author Fran Migliaccio of feelings of someone's hands touching her, as well as an experience of disembodiment, as though a spirit was channeling its energy through her.

Whatever spirits reside in the Highview, the hotel has a long and storied history, being the second-longest continuously operating hotel since 1878, when M.M. Davis opened its doors. Presidents, the White House marching band and celebrities of all kinds stayed at the Highview during the Gilded Age. Later in the century, another legacy of a kind was to be created in the hotel when the itinerant artist H.D. Wetherbee came to the island as a guest of Captain Gene Stinson in the late 1940s. According to locals, Wetherbee painted the murals of island life that adorn the guest rooms and the bar in exchange for room and board and a bottle of scotch a day.

Sadly, the beautiful scenes of Old Harbor and the sparse landscapes of the western side of the island that were still common scenes on Block Island in the forties are the only artistic legacy of a man who died homeless in New York in the 1980s. One might well wish that it was poor Weatherbee ringing the chimes in the old hotel, back on the island he loved.

On New Shoreham's Old Town Road lies a modest ten-room inn that dates from 1825 and rests at the crossroads of what was once a bustling center of commerce on the island. In the 1870s, the building was the home and site of a general store opened by Lorenzo Littlefield. Ledgers from the time show that the merchant sold all manner of goods in the store, from boots to blackstrap molasses. The house later belonged to Frank and Lily Littlefield and stayed in the family until it was sold in the 1980s and turned into an inn.

A descendant of the Littlefields told the story that Lily had died in the house, and for a long time, it had been rumored that she was pushed down the stairs. Ann Elizabeth Littlefield did, in fact, die in the house, and for a time, her son Frank, then a state senator, was a suspect, but the case was never solved. No one in the family is certain that the rumors were true, but it might explain the apparition seen one afternoon that Johno Sisto, the owner of the island's bookstore and press, as well as a two-term town councilman, experienced as he drove by the Old Town Inn.

As he turned his car around the bend coming up toward the inn, he noticed a woman walking from the front door of the inn towards the road. This might not seem unusual at all, but the inn had been closed for a year or more, and the woman was dressed in

> Edwardian-era clothes, something you would see in a Masterpiece Theater series. She had brown hair pulled up in a bun, and she was wearing a white blouse with a high neck and ruffled sleeves and a dark red jumper…She wore black boots. She was walking very purposefully with straight, measured steps, holding her hands together in front of her and looking down. As I passed her and began slowing down, coming up to the stop sign, she turned and started walking toward the large horse chestnut tree that stands at the corner of the property next to the intersection. She never took any notice of me.[47]

When he stopped at the intersection and looked back toward the inn, the apparition had disappeared, and Sisto drove on toward home, certain from that day on that he had seen a ghost.

Another well-known islander recalled a similar experience that took place in the house on Sunset Hill, which Edrie Dodge and her husband, Will, ran as a bed-and-breakfast when they retired. The incident happened when she was a girl of twenty-five and sitting with her mother in the living room of the house. She recalled that

I glanced over at the rocker, and I saw a man sitting there. He was a stranger, and he was wearing a black suit...I'd never seen this person before, and I haven't seen him since, but I remember just how he looked. He was tall and thin, with a thin face and high cheekbones. He had dark hair that was shiny and slicked down as if it had been greased. I got a strange feeling, just looking at him.

No one had entered the room, or even knocked on the door, so far as she'd noticed. Edrie asked her mother if she could see the man in the rocking chair. When she was told that there was no one else in the room as far as her mother could tell, she asked her to look closely at the rocker, and sure enough, her mother could see that it was moving, though she could see no one there. Edrie, however, could still plainly see the man in the black suit. She guessed now that she was seeing a ghost and recalled an old truism given her by her Aunt Mabel that when you see a ghost, you're supposed to ask them what they want. So she turned to the ghost and asked him. "That man turned toward me when I said that," she recalled, "and just grinned at me—a great big grin, from ear to ear—and just kept looking at me, with this grin on his face. I didn't know what to make of it. But I just kept looking back at him, and finally I said, 'I think you're in the wrong place.'"

And with that, the man in the black suit vanished.

Chapter 7

THE TAVERN RESTORED

With the advent of the trolley car and railroad, the taverns that were relied on so long as rest stops for the individual traveler or those in stagecoaches along the old routes soon saw a rapid decline in business. This decline, along with the rise of temperance movements across the country, led many of these public houses to close their doors. Some became private homes, others still maintained business for a time, but many were abandoned and fell into disrepair. These often became victims of fire, the age-old scourge of our early wooden homes, or to the wrecking ball as urban expansion and planning razed much of Providence's historic buildings before the days of preservation.

Often, there was much more lost than the inns and taverns themselves when such a catastrophe occurred. As illustrated by historian Ann Eckert Brown, when the muralist Rufus Porter visited Providence in 1822, he took a room at the Wesson Coffee House and an advertisement in the *Providence Gazette*, offering his services in "Landscape Scenery, at prices less than the ordinary expence of papering."

Porter traveled throughout New England during his career and painted many scenes in ordinary houses, as well as taverns and inns, that are well prized today and collected in the museum that bears his namesake in Bridgton, Maine.

His advertisement in late November addressed "those Gentlemen who are desirous of spending the gloomy winter months amidst pleasant groves and verdant fields, are respectfully invited to apply above, where a specimen of the work may be seen."[48]

Photograph of a Boston–Providence railway car, circa 1840. *Courtesy of the Rhode Island Historical Society.*

Unfortunately, the mural left by Porter was destroyed by the fire that razed the house in 1852.

THE MOWRY TAVERN RESTORED

One of the first taverns to be restored in Rhode Island was the Roger Mowry Tavern, the oldest in Providence (see Chapter 3). Writing in 1895, Norman Isham describes the house after restoration:

> *This house, as the visitor approaches it along Abbott street, up the hill from North Main gives no impression of its age. From above it, looking back, we see the old stone chimney which though topped out with brick is almost exactly in its ancient condition, and which shows, on its sides, the shoulders or slopes which mark the position of the rafters of the original roof.*[49]

As an architect and historian, Isham had a keen eye for these signs of age and the handiwork of the early Providence builder William Carpenter, who erected many of those early houses that "thickly fringed" the old town street, as well as the masonry of the stone-enders and tall chimneys that were often

Sketch of the Roger Mowry House from Norman Isham and Albert F. Brown's *Early Rhode Island Houses* (1895). *Photo by James Allen.*

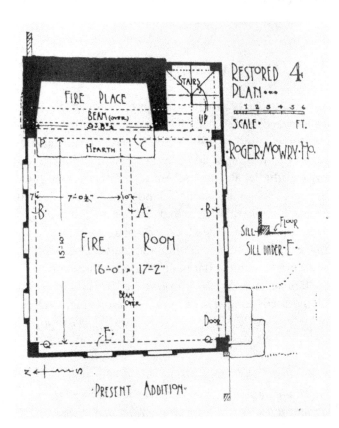

Sketch of "Restored Section" of the Mowry House from Norman Isham and Albert F. Brown's *Early Rhode Island Houses* (1895). *Photo by James Allen.*

the work of John Smith, another early craftsman of Rhode Island. Isham noted with admiration that "it is inside the building…that its age can best be appreciated."

Inside the old tavern, Isham found that although the house had been much altered over the years, the original posts and beams, including the "summer tree," remained intact, as did the enormous fireplace, though at the time of his restoration, he wrote that

> *the present arrangement of the room would not lead the visitor to suspect the size or even the existence of the old stone fireplace. There is a fire-board behind the stove, and on each side of the fire-board a closet. Opening one of the closet doors however, will reveal the stone cavern wherein, when the Town Council met, Roger Mowry burnt the logs of "this daies firing."[50]*

It was this original part of the house that Isham restored, though sadly, less than a decade later in 1900, the tavern would be razed to build a three-story tenement.

THE OLD PIDGE HOUSE

Around this time, another ancient tavern nearby faced a similar fate. The Old Pidge House as it was called, was sold in 1901 after James Pidge's death. And then sold again to the railroad in 1905 when it was certain that the old house would be taken down. But it didn't happen. As mentioned in a previous chapter, efforts by the local Franco-American Society may have altered the railroad's plans once the Rhode Island and local historical societies became involved. The likely truth is that no one really wanted to tear the old tavern down. As the years passed, time seemed to progress only around the old building. Even as a Texaco station and factories grew along Pawtucket Avenue, the tavern remained, but in an ever declining state.

When Granville S. Standish bought the property in 1922, there was a glimmer of hope that the seeds long-sewn for preservation might finally come to fruition. On December 22, 1922, the *Providence Journal* reported optimistically that

> *Reconstruction work on the Old Pidge House, one of Pawtucket's oldest and most treasured historical landmarks…is rapidly nearing completion…The house, a two story wooden structure, was fast falling*

Old Pidge House in decline, circa 1905. *Courtesy of the Johnson research files, Pawtucket Public Library.*

The Old Pidge House after restoration, circa 1940. *Photo by Frank Farley. Courtesy of the Johnson Research file, Pawtucket Public Library.*

into decay until the work of reclaiming it was started. The dwelling, in its dilapidated condition, was the source of continual criticism by members of various organizations in Pawtucket.

The article continues to mention that, in October of that year,

a squad of men, under the direction of the present owners, set out to repair the building. Broken window frames were replaced. The roof, which had been minus many of its shingles has been recovered. The four walls, which evidenced the ravages of time, have been straightened. The exterior has been lathed with new stripe.

The old chimney that warmed the lower chamber and the upstairs rooms was also patched and repaired.

The photo here (circa 1940) shows the house some years after restoration. Every effort was made by Standish to promote the house as a living museum. In 1924, the old tavern was featured in the published collection of George D. Laswell's *Corners and Characters of Rhode Island*. In 1932, Standish commissioned local artist Lyman Slocum to sketch the historic house and its interior, and these illustrations were used in promotional materials and published in a calendar as well.

Philip D. Greer, an ardent preservationist in Providence, was instrumental in listing the house with the Historic American Buildings Survey and in later obtaining a marker that designated the tavern as an historic sight along the old Post Road.

Despite these efforts, the house remained in private hands, and upon Standish's death in 1953, the fight to save the Old Pidge House came to an end. Within months, the late preservationist's own company had erected huge billboards in the front and on the side of the massive structure, and then it slowly began dismantling what had been a mainstay at the junction for over three hundred years.

On March 28, 1954, the *Providence Journal* reported that "behind the billboards, the stout frame structure is falling in ruins. The carved doorway has been removed, and the vast central chimney, which provided a fireplace for every room, has largely disappeared."

Before the wrecking ball, however, the entire interior of the taproom, the stairway and an upstairs chamber were carefully removed and reconstructed in the executive wing of the Standish Barnes building at India Point.

A former sales representative with the company remembers the day he first opened the door of the old tavern and stepped inside the taproom. "It was just like somebody had set down the last glass and closed the door," he told the author, and he can distinctly recall the reconstructed rooms and the artifacts brought with them. Included with the old panels and moulding from the walls, there was the old liquor license on the wall, and a long table made from the door.

Within years, the company had closed its offices in Rhode Island, and in 1962, the Standish-Barnes building was torn down. Only recently did it come to light that the room was dismantled once again and has remained in storage for over fifty years. The former employee is certain that many of the artifacts must also remain in someone's possession and harbors a longtime wish to obtain the license and reopen the Old Pidge Tavern.

Over time, it became clear that as long as these old buildings remained in private hands, there was a danger of losing them to posterity. Those owners who cared about preserving the history of their houses began to donate them to organizations who would take the necessary steps to ensure their continued existence.

THE ELEAZER ARNOLD HOUSE

One such owner was Preserved Whipple Arnold, the last descendant in a long line to own the Eleazer Arnold House, described in our first chapter. The house had operated as a tavern until 1902 and, after some years of disuse, was given by Arnold to the Society for the Preservation of New England Antiquities in 1919.

A year later, the society hired preservationist Norman M. Isham to inspect and direct a stabilization of the building. Isham was familiar with the house. He had included a description with sketches in his *Early Rhode Island Houses (1895)*:

> *This picturesque dwelling—built in 1687 by Eleazer Arnold—stands on the old North road, half a mile this side of the Butterfly Factory, and about a mile west of Lonsdale…The house differs from any we have thus far studied. It was originally built, as the old slope of the chimney shows, with a lean-to…But here the lean-to is not a sleeping-room or a mere store-room. The chimney, as can be seen from the perspective and the plan, extended across the whole end of the house on the outside; the lean-to became the kitchen and had its own fireplace like its more aristocratic neighbor, the old fire-room.*

The Eleazer Arnold House after restoration. *Photo by author.*

The Tavern Restored

Front view of the Eleazer Arnold House. *Photo by author.*

About the time of Isham's stabilization of the old house, another old tavern that had been donated to the society was moved to the site from Pawtucket. The Croade Tavern had been built in 1700 and, as it was a far less imposing structure than the Arnold House, was electrified and used as an office for those involved in the restoration.

In 1950, a decidedly more ambitious restoration project was undertaken. The society had decided to remove the later alterations that had been made to the house and return the building to its seventeenth-century appearance. Many of the early architectural pieces of the house were missing and had to be fabricated by hand. These included the tiny, diamond-paned casement windows that originally adorned the building, as well as the interior paneling and a plain wooden door.

The building is now part of the Blackstone River Valley National Heritage Corridor, along with Hearthside, Chase Farm, Hoffit Mill and other early Rhode Island structures that have been preserved along Great Road in Lincoln. The Arnold House and Croade Tavern are owned by Historic New England, which continues its efforts to maintain a number of historic houses throughout New England.

THE RESOLVE WATERMAN TAVERN/
SMITHFIELD EXCHANGE BANK

One of the more recent and community-wide efforts of preservation involved the Resolve Waterman Tavern that sits in the old village center of Greenville, Rhode Island. This is the tavern briefly mentioned in Chapter 1, built in 1733 and then expanded with two ells in 1822, one of which became the Smithfield Exchange Bank. The bank remained in the tavern until 1856, when it moved into a brick building next door. The tavern operated until 1902. The main structure of the tavern was demolished in 1936 when the Pike was expanded, and the remaining ells were modified to stand alone. A new façade was built, and the two-storied, gabled structure was a private residence until 1969.

For the next thirty-nine years, the building was allowed to deteriorate. Cumberland Farms had purchased the property from the last private owners, but it was not until 2003 that the company donated the property to the town in exchange for tax credits. The initial efforts to preserve the building were begun by the Smithfield Historic Preservation Society, and this eventually led, in 2006, to the Smithfield Exchange Bank being listed on the National Register of Historic Places and the forming of a group solely dedicated to the restoration project, known as the Smithfield Preservation Society.

By 2009, the group of community conservationists had secured funds of $50,000 from the Gregson Foundation, as well as a $10,000 donation from Masonic Temple Lodge No. 18, which was once housed down the street from the tavern.

With these donations, as well as the labor and materials donated or provided at discount by local businesses, architect Richard Leach told the *Smithfield Valley Breeze* that the society could now paint and clapboard three sides of the structure, shingle the roof in cedar, rebuild the chimney and restore the windows.

The second phase of restoration focused on the building's interior, which to the State's Historic Preservation and Heritage Commission, was a local treasure:

> *Inside…the second floor reveals the building's history as a bank. The walls and ceiling are unadorned plaster; the floors are wide wood planks. A long wall separates the space into two large rooms. The Director's Room, on the west side, was where bank officials held meetings. The room's cove-ceiling, Federal mantle, and molded chair rail mark it as a formal space. The Banking Hall is located on the east side, and mortices in the floor (and patterns of wear on the floorboards) suggest*

The Resolve Waterman Tavern/Smithfield Bank Exchange after restoration. *Photo by author.*

that a banking counter was once located at the northern end of this space,
separating the customers from the cashier and the Bank Vault. The
Bank Vault is a three-foot-square masonry enclosure located on the north
wall and incorporated into the masonry of the chimney. Used to store
paper currency and specie, the vault is sheathed with narrow, wrought-
iron plates bolted to the stonework. The outer doorway is composed of
monolithic granite posts and a heavy lintel, and the inner wrought-iron
plate door remains in place.[51]

Fully restored, the Exchange has become the focal point of teaching
local history to the town's schoolchildren and a place of meetings and
functions for the society that maintains the building. It is also a source
of pride for those residents who finally succeeded in having the historic
tavern and bank restored after years of passersby seeing nothing but a
deteriorated wooden shell of what was once the hub of the town. The
Smithfield Exchange had financed many of the local dam projects that
allowed mills and power-driven factories to grow in town as Rhode Island
began the industrial age.

The recent care and restoration of these old houses reflect the ongoing respect that each generation has found among its members of diverse backgrounds. In Rhode Island, the generations of people who have worked to restore and preserve the old taverns and houses have been historians, anthropologists and architects but also masons, builders and painters, like those who autographed the beams in the attic of the Eleazor Arnold house: G.A. Hayes, painter, and G.T. Leonard in 1876; F.M. Crystal in 1902; L. Havey and E.J. Healey in 1911; P. Patry in 1942; J.S. Johnson 1951; and Beth and John C. Zangari, as well as P.L. Zangari of later restorations.

In recent years, the expense of running a house as a "living museum" has become prohibitive, and many of these protected places are now reduced to opening only a few hours a month and keeping just a small staff to maintain the building. Government grants have benefited some historic areas, such as the aforementioned Blackstone River Valley Corridor, in which Great Road rambles from the intersection of Smithfield Avenue to the old George Washington Highway.

The future of other houses remains uncertain, however, as the historical societies and organizations entrusted to their care face dwindling donations and rely largely on volunteers to provide tours and maintenance. Those of us who treasure these places must see that they are not forgotten, and to that end, I hope this book does its part.

To lose these old houses and taverns would be to lose not only the physical structure but also the palpable sense of history that exists with the structure. Lost would be the sense of the strength it took to clear a piece of wilderness and build such a house and the courage to lay claim to such freedoms, a trait that Rhode Islanders still see today as an inherent part of their being.

NOTES

CHAPTER 1

1. *Early Records of Providence*, Providence Record Commissioners, 1916.
2. Deetz, *Small Things Forgotten*, 107.
3. Chapin, *Early Records of Rhode Island*.
4. Salinger, *Taverns and Drinking in Early America*, 144.
5. Chapin, *Documentary History of Rhode Island*.
6. Deetz cites the availability of wood to build such a structure as the probable cause of design, yet other sources maintain that the extended portion of the house was almost always the "brew-room" and as such was "removed" from the main part of the house in case of fire or accident.
7. *Pawtucket Times*.
8. The newspaper reported that her body was found beneath a table in the charred remains by her longtime friend and local fireman Joseph Paradise. It's said that her loyal dog was found at her side.
9. Bridenbaugh, *Gentlemen's Progess*, 150.
10. Bridenbaugh, *Cities in the Wilderness*, 273.
11. Carpenter, *South County Studies*, 238.
12. McBurney, *A History of Kingston*, 30.
13. Ibid., 29.
14. Greene, *Pursuits of Happiness*, 67.
15. Report of the Historic Preservation Society on the city of Johnston.
16. Jenks, *Dwellings in Northeastern Rhode Island and the Smithfields*.
17. Quoted in Field, *The Colonial Tavern*.

Chapter 2

18. Earle, *Stage-Coach and Tavern Days*.
19. Smith, *Beer in America*.
20. Baron, *Brewed in America*, 82.
22. Journal of Grant Thorburn, quoted in Earle's *Stage-Coach and Tavern Days*, 72.
23. Salinger, *Taverns and Drinking in Early America*, 57.
24. Belcher, "Pictures of Providence."
25. I am indebted to the hospitality of Natalie King, present owner of the house where the Kings Arms Tavern once held business. Mrs. King has restored the house's eighteenth-century interior and fireplaces after alterations by the previous owner, and she proudly displays a replica of the original tavern sign painted by her son. Mrs. King was kind enough to give me and my wife a tour of the main floor.

Chapter 3

26. Also spelled "Clauson" in more modern accounts. I have used the spelling as it appeared in the Early Records of Providence and in the letters of Roger Williams.
27. Letter from Roger Williams in defense of his acquisition of Clawson's estate after his death to the Court of Providence Plantations, May 11, 1661
28. In Edward Field's inventory, we find "a froe, an iron bench hook, hammer, inch and 1/2 auger, inch auger, narrow axe, 'hallowing' plane, a broad chisel, a sloape pynted chisel, a gouge for carpenters works, a pearing chisel, a little hammer, a three square file, two cold punches, three brest wimble bittes, the biggest, the middlemost, the least bitt, and a whetstone."
29. Spelled various ways in the different versions of the story, this is Field's spelling in his *History of Providence Plantations*.
30. *Early Records of Providence*, 70.
31. Letter from Roger Williams to Court of Providence, May 1661.
32. Field, *The Colonial Taverns*, 212.

Chapter 4

33. I am indebted to Dennis Landis of the John Carter Brown Library for this quote as a starting point to this chapter. It was included in his talk "Fair and Balanced? The German Press and the American War 1776" at the JCB Luncheon on March 23, 2011.

34. *Providence Gazette*, March 28, 1772.

35. Newsletter of the Warwick Historical Society, May 1990.

36. *The Gaspee Room*, pamphlet published by Old Stone Bank, 1931.

37. Quoted from Bicknell, *History of Rhode Island*, 300.

38. Collins, "Pictures of Providence."

39. Rau, "Sergeant John Smith's Diary," 249–50.

40. Ibid., 13.

CHAPTER 5

41. Mowry, *The Dorr War*, 68.

42. Ibid.

43. Ibid., 338.

44. Conley, "No Tempest in a Teapot."

CHAPTER 6

45. *Handbook of Historical Sites.*

46. Migliaccio, *Block Island Ghosts*, 59.

47. Ibid., 99–100.

CHAPTER 7

48. From Brown's *American Painted Floors*, 59.

49. Isham and Brown, *Early Rhode Island Houses*, 21.

50. Ibid., 22.

51. Description taken from the press release of the Rhode Island Historical Preservation and Heritage Commission on May 6, 2006.

BIBLIOGRAPHY

Baron, Stanley Wade. *Brewed in America: A History of Beer and Ale in the United States*. N.p.: Ayer Company Publications, 1972.

Bayles, Richard M. *History of Providence County* Vols. 1–2. New York: W.W. Preston and Company, 1891.

Belcher, Horace. "Mr. Tambo and Mr. Bones." *Rhode Island Historical Society Bulletin* (October 1949).

———. "The Old Hoyle Tavern." *Rhode Island Historical Society Bulletin* 12 and 13 (1935).

———. "Pictures of Providence in the Past." *Rhode Island Historical Society Bulletin* (1935–1936).

———. "Taverns of Pawtuxet." Unpublished, Warwick Historical Society.

Bicknell, Thomas. *The History of the State of Rhode Island and Providence Plantations*. Providence, RI: American Historical Society, 1920.

Bray, Robert, and Paul Bushnell. *Diary of a Common Soldier in the American Revolution 1775–1783: An Annotated Edition of the Military Journal of Jeremiah Greenman*. DeKalb: Northern Illinois University Press, 1978.

Bridenbaugh, Carl. *Cities in the Wilderness*. New York: Knopf, 1955.

Bridenbaugh, Carl, ed. *Gentlemen's Progess: The Itinerarium of Alexander Hamilton*. Providence: Brown University Press, 1948.

Brown, Ann Eckert. *American Painted Floors Before 1840*. Rhode Island: Spring Green Books, 2008.

Carpenter, Esther Bernon. *South County Studies of Some Eighteenth Century Persons, Places and Conditions*. N.p.: Ayer Publishing, 1924.

Chapin, Howard. *Documentary History of Rhode Island*. Providence: Rhode Island Historical Society, 1938.

———. *The Early Records of Rhode Island*. Providence: Rhode Island Historical Society, 1938.

Collins, Clarkeson A., III, ed. "Pictures of Providence in the Past: 1790–1820: The Reminiscences of Walter R. Danforth." *Rhode Island Historical Society Bulletin* 10, no. 1.

Conley, Patrick. "No Tempest in a Teapot." *Rhode Island Historical Society Bulletin* 50, no. 3.

Crawford, Mary Caroline. *Little Pilgrimages Among Old New England Inns*. Boston: C.L. Page and Company, 1907.

D'Agostino, Thomas. *A Guide to Haunted New England*. Charleston, SC: The History Press, 2009.

D'Amato, Donald. *Warwick's Villages: Glimpses of the Past*. Charleston, SC: The History Press, 2009.

Deetz, James. *In Small Things Forgotten: The Archeology of Early American Life*. New York: Anchor Books, 1977.

Earle, Alice Morse. *Stage-Coach and Tavern Days*. New York: MacMillan Company, 1900.

Early Records of the Town of Providence. Vol. 1. Providence Record Commissioners, 1916.

Field, Edward. *The Colonial Tavern*. Providence, RI: Preston and Rounds, 1897.

———. *State of Rhode Island and Providence Plantations at the End of the Century*. Vols. 1–4. Boston: Mason Publishing, 1902.

Geake, Robert A. *A Toll, a Tavern, and a Farm*. Providence: RIfootprints press, 2009.

Greene, Jack P. *Pursuits of Happiness*. Chapel Hill: University of North Carolina, 1988.

Handbook of Historical Sites in Rhode Island. Providence, RI: Dept. of Public Schools, 1936.

Isham, Norman, and Albert F. Brown. *Early Rhode Island Houses: An Historical and Architectural Study*.

Jenks, Grover L. *Dwellings in Northeastern Rhode Island and the Smithfields*. N.p.: Kessinger Publishing, reprinted 2010.

Knight, Sarah Kemble. *The Journal of Madam Knight*. N.p.: American Book Company, 1938.

Lancaster, Jane. "By the Pens of Females: Rhode Island Teenage Girls' Diaries, 1788–1821." *Rhode Island History* 57, nos. 3–4 (1999).

McBurney, Christian. *A History of Kingston, R.I., 1700–1900*. Kingston, RI: Pettasquamscutt Historical Society, 2004.

————. *The Rhode Island Campaign.* Yardley, PA: Westholme Publishing, 2011.

Migliaccio, Fran. *Block Island Ghosts.* Rhode Island: self-published, 2005.

Mowry, Arthur May. *The Dorr War or The Constitution Struggle in Rhode Island.* Providence: Preston and Rounds, 1901.

Mullins, Lisa C., ed. *Early Architecture of Rhode Island.* Harrisburg, PA: National Historical Society, 1987.

Old Stone Bank. *The Gaspee Room.* Pamphlet published in 1931.

Rau, Louise, ed. "Sergeant John Smith's Diary of 1776." *The Mississippi Valley Historical Review* 10 (1933).

Raven, Rory. *The Dorr War: Treason, Rebellion and the Fight for Reform in Rhode Island.* Charleston, SC: The History Press, 2010.

Records of the Court Trials of Rhode Island and Providence Plantations. Vol. 1. Rhode Island Historical Society, 1920.

Salinger, Susan V. *Taverns and Drinking in Early America.* Baltimore, MD: Johns Hopkins University Press, 2004.

Smith, Greg. *Beer in America: The Early Years 1587–1840.* Boulder, CO: Brewer Publications, 1998.

Zwicker, Roxie J. *Haunted Pubs of New England.* Charleston, SC: The History Press, 2007.

WEBSITES

Chepachet Free Will Baptist Church. http://www.chepachetfreewill.org.

Tavern Life. http://www.blanchardstavern.org.

Town of Smithfield, Rhode Island, history. http://www.smithfieldri.com.

White Horse Tavern Ghost Stories. http://www.quahog.org.

INDEX

INDEX

ABOUT THE AUTHOR

Photo by William G. Geake III.

Robert A. Geake is a local historian and author whose previous books include *A History of the Narragansett Tribe of Rhode Island: Keepers of the Bay*, from The History Press, and *A Toll, a Tavern and a Farm*, printed for the Pawtucket Preservation Society.

Mr. Geake is an associate of the John Carter Brown Library at Brown University and a member of the Rhode Island Historical Society. He has lived for nearly thirty years in the farmhouse that James Pidge built in 1860, just above his tavern on the Post Road, and Mr. Geake is the home-brewer of "Old Pidge Ales."